Fidel Castro Speaks

Title: Fidel Castro Speaks

ISBN-13: 978-1-942825-34-0

Author: Kambiz Mostofizadeh

Publisher: Mikazuki Publishing House

Description: This book explores the ideas of Fidel Castro of Cuba.

Fidel Castro Speaks

Fidel Castro Speech in Santiago

Compatriots of All Cuba, We have finally reached Santiago de Cuba. The road was long and difficult, but we finally arrived. It was rumored that they expected us in the capital of the Republic at 2 p.m. today. No one was more amazed by this than I, because I was the first one to be surprised by this treacherous blow, which would place me in the capital of the Republic this morning. Moreover, I intended to be in the capital of the Republic -- that is, in the new capital of the Republic -- because Santiago de Cuba, in accordance with the wishes of the Provisional President, in accordance with the wishes of the Rebel Army, and in accordance with the wishes of the people of Santiago de Cuba, who really deserved it, Santiago will be the new capital of Cuba. Santiago de Cuba will be the provisional capital of the Republic. This measure may surprise some people. Admittedly, it is new, but the revolution is characterized precisely by its newness, by the fact that it will do things that have never been done before. The Revolution Begins Now In making Santiago de Cuba the provisional capital of the Republic, we are fully aware of our reason for doing so. This is no attempt to cajole a specific area by

Fidel Castro Speaks

demogogic means. It is simply that Santiago de Cuba has been the strongest bulwark of the revolution, a revolution that is beginning now. Our Revolution will be no easy task, but a harsh and dangerous undertaking, particularly in the initial phases. And in what better place could we establish the Government of the Republic than in this fortress of the Revolution. So that you may know that this will be a government solidly supported by the people of this heroic city, located in the foothills of the Sierra Maestra -- because Santiago de Cuba is a part of the Sierra Maestra -- Santiago de Cuba and the Sierra Maestra will provide the two strongest fortresses for the Revolution. However, there are other reasons that motivate us, and one is the military revolutionary movement, the truly military revolutionary movement which did not take place in Colombia. The Puny Little Uprising of Colombia In Colombia they prepared a puny little uprising against the revolution, principally with Batista's assistance. Since it is necessary to tell the truth and since we came here with a view to orienting people, I can tell you and I can assure you that the military uprising in Colombia was an attempt to deprive the people in power, to rob the revolution of its triumph and to allow

Fidel Castro Speaks

Batista to escape, to allow the Tabernilla to escape, to allow the Tabernillas to escape together with the Pilar Garcias, to allow the Salas Canizares and the Venturas. The Colombian uprising was an ambitious and treacherous blow that deserves the lowest epithets. We must call a spade a spade and put the blame where it belongs. I am not going to be diplomatic. I will say outright that General Cantillo betrayed us and not only am I going to say it, but I am going to prove it to you. However, we had always said so. We had always said that there would be no point in resolving this matter at the last moment with a puny little military uprising, because if there is a military uprising, concealed from the people, our Revolution will go forward nonetheless and this time cannot be over the power. It will not be like 1895 when the Americans came and took over, intervening at the last moment, and afterwards did not even allow Calixto Garcia to assume leadership, although he had fought at Santiago de Cuba for 30 years. Nor will it be like 1933, when the people began to believe that the revolution was going to triumph, and Mr. Batista came in to betray the revolution, take over power, and establish an 11-year-long

Fidel Castro Speaks

dictatorship. Neither Treason nor Intervention Nor will it be like 1944, when the people took courage, believing that they had finally reached a position where they could take over the power, while those who did assume power proved to be thieves. We will have no thievery, no treason, no intervention. This time it is truly the revolution, even though some might not desire it. At the very moment that the dictatorship fell, as a consequence of the military victories of our Revolution, when they could not hold out even another 15 days, Mr. Cantillo appears on the scene as a paladin of freedom. Naturally, we have never been remiss in refusing any offer of collaboration that might prevent bloodshed, providing the aims of our Revolution were not imperiled thereby. Naturally, we have always appealed to the military in our search for peace, but it must be peace for freedom and peace with the triumph of our Revolution. This is the only way to obtain peace. Hence, on December 24, when we were told of General Cantillo's desire to meet us, we agreed to the interview. And I must confess to you that, given the course of events, the extraordinary development of our military operations, I had very little interest in speaking of military movements. Nevertheless, I

Fidel Castro Speaks

felt that it was the duty of those of us with responsibility not to allow ourselves to be carried away by our feelings. I also thought that if triumph could be achieved with the minimum bloodshed, it was my duty to listen to the proposals made by the military. To Prevent Batista's Flight I went to meet Mr. Cantillo, who spoke to me on behalf of the Army. He met me on the 28th (December) at the Oriente mill, where he arrived in a helicopter at 8 p.m. We talked for four hours and I will not invent any stories about what took place, since there were several exceptional witnesses to the interview. There was Dr. Raul Chibas, there was a Catholic priest, there were several military men, whose evidence cannot be questioned on any grounds whatsoever. After analyzing all of Cuba's problems, and underlining all the minute details, General Cantillo agreed to carry out a military revolutionary movement with us. The first thing I said to him was this: After carefully studying the situation, the situation of the Army, the situation in which it had been placed by the dictatorship, after explaining to him that he did not have to concern himself with Batista, nor with the Tabernillas, nor with the rest of those people because none of them had shown any

Fidel Castro Speaks

concern for the Cuban military forces, we
showed him that those people had lead the
military into a campaign against the masses, a
campaign that can never be victorious because
no one can win a war against the mass of the
population. After telling him that the military
forces were the victims of the regime's
immorality, that the budgetary allocations for the
purchase of arms were embezzled, that the
soldiers were being constantly defrauded, that
those people did not deserve the consideration
of honorable military men, that the Army had no
reason to bear the blame for crimes committed
by Batista's gangs of villains, I told him quite
clearly that I did not authorize any type of
movement that would enable Batista to escape.
I warned him that if Batista got away afterwards
with the Tabernillas and the rest of them it would
be because we had been unable to prevent it.
We had to prevent Batista's flight. The People
Obtain Their Freedom by Conquest Everyone
knows that our first requirement in the event of a
military uprising -- that is, a military uprising in
conjunction with our movement -- was the
surrender of the war criminals. This is an
essential condition. We could have captured
Batista and all his accomplices and I said it

Fidel Castro Speaks

loudly and clearly that I was not in agreement
with Batista's escape. I explained to him quite
clearly what course of action would have to be
taken and that I did not give any support (to
Batista's escape) nor would the 27th of July
Movement, nor would the people support a coup
d'etat (on such terms), because the fact is that it
was the people who obtained their freedom by
conquest and only the people who did it. Our
freedom was taken from us by a coup d'etat but
in order to finish once and for all with coups
d'etat, it was necessary to achieve freedom by
dint of the people's sacrifice. We could achieve
nothing by one uprising today and another
tomorrow and another two years later and
another three years after, because here in Cuba
it is the people, and the people alone, who must
decide who is to govern them. The military
forces must unconditionally obey the people's
orders and be at the disposal of the people, of
the constitution and of the Laws of the Republic.
If there is a poor government that embezzles
and does more than four wrong things, the only
thing to do is to wait a little while and when
election time comes the bad government is
turned out of office. That is why in democratic,
constitutional regimes governments have a fixed

Fidel Castro Speaks

mandate. If they are bad, they can be ousted by the people, who can vote for a better government. The function of the military is not to elect governments, but to guarantee laws and to guarantee the rights of the citizens. That is why I warned him that a coup d'etat was out of the question, but a military revolutionary movement was in order and it should take place in Santiago de Cuba and not in Colombia. An Unkept Promise I told him quite clearly that the only way of forming a link with the people and joining them, of uniting the military and the revolutionaries was not a coup d'etat in the early hours of the dawn in Colombia -- at 2 or 3 a.m. -- about which no one would know anything, as is the usual practice of the gentlemen. I told him it would be necessary to arouse the garrison at Santiago de Cuba, which was quite strong and adequately armed, in order to start the military movement, which would then be joined by the people and the revolutionaries. Given the situation in which the dictatorship found itself, such movement would prove irresistible because all the other garrisons in the country would certainly join it at once. That was what was agreed upon and not only was it what was agreed upon but I made him promise it. He

Fidel Castro Speaks

intended to go to Havana the next day and we did not agree with this. I said to him, "It is risky for you to go to Havana." And he replied, "No, no there is no risk in it." I insisted, "You are running a great risk of arrest because if there is a conspiracy, everyone knows about it here." "No, I am sure they will not arrest me," he replied. And, of course, why would they arrest him if this was a "coup d'etat of Batista?" My thoughts were, "Well, all this seems so easy that it might well be a suspicious movement," so I said to him, "Will you promise me that in Havana you will not be persuaded by those interests which support you to carry out a coup d'etat in the capital? Will you promise me that you will not do it? His reply was, "I promise I won't." I insisted, "Will you swear to me that you won't?" And his reply again, "I swear I won't!" A Dive into Space I believe that the prime requisite for a military man is honor, that the prime requisite of a military man is his word. This gentleman not only proved that he is dishonorable and that his word is worth nothing, but that he also lacks intelligence. I say this because a movement which could have been organized from the start with the support of the whole population, with its victory assured from

Fidel Castro Speaks

the outset, did nothing more than dive into space. He believed that it would be only too easy to fool the people and to mislead the Revolution. He knew some things. He knew, for instance, that when we told the people that Batista had got hold of a plane the people would flock into the streets, madly happy. They thought that the people were not sufficiently mature to distinguish between Batista's flight and the Revolution. Because if Batista goes and over there Cantillo's friends assume command, it is quite likely that Dr. Urrutia would also have to go within three months. Because just as they were betraying us now, so would they betray us later and the truth of the matter is that Mr. Cantillo betrayed us before the Revolution. He gave signs of this and I can prove it. We agreed with General Cantillo that the uprising would take place on the 31st at 3 p.m. and it was agreed that the armed forces would give unconditional support to the revolutionary movement. The President was to appoint the revolutionary leaders and establish the positions to which the revolutionary leaders would assign the military. They were offering unconditional support and every detail of the plan was agreed upon. At 3 p.m. on the 31st the garrison at

Fidel Castro Speaks

Santiago de Cuba was to rise in revolt. Immediately after several rebel columns would enter the city and the people would fraternize with the military and the rebels, immediately submitting a revolutionary proclamation to the country as a whole and calling on all honorable military men to join the movement. It was agreed that the talks in the city would be placed at our disposal and I personally offered to advance toward the capital with an armed column preceded by the tanks. The tanks in the city would be placed at our disposal and I personally offered to advance toward the capital with an armed column preceded by the tanks. The tanks were to be handed to me at 3 p.m., not because it was felt that any fighting would be necessary but only against the possibility that in Havana the Movement might fail, making it necessary to place our vanguard as close as possible to the capital and to prevent any such occurrences in Havana. Cantillo's Responsibility It was evident that with the hatred for the public forces created by the horrendous crimes committed by Ventura and Pilar Garcia, Batista's fall would create considerable upheaval among the people. Moreover, the police force would inevitably feel that it lacked

Fidel Castro Speaks

the moral strength to contain the populace, as in fact happened. A series of excesses were recorded in the capital. There was looting, shooting, fires, and all the responsibility for it falls on the shoulders of General Cantillo, who betrayed his word of honor, who failed to carry out the plan which had been agreed upon. He believed that by appointing police captains and commanders, many of whom had already deserted when they were appointed -- proof that they had a guilty conscience -- would be enough to solve the problem. How different things were in Santiago de Cuba! How orderly and civic-minded! How disciplined the behavior of the masses! There was not a single attempt to loot, not a single example of personal vengeance, not a single man dragged through the streets, not a single fire! The behavior of the population of Santiago de Cuba was admirable and exemplary despite two factors. One of these was that Santiago de Cuba was the city which had suffered the most, where there had been the greatest terrorism and where, consequently, one would expect the people to be indignant. Moreover, despite our statements of this morning that we were not in agreement with the coup d'etat, the population in Santiago de Cuba

Fidel Castro Speaks

behaved in an exemplary fashion.... (A typing error makes the translation of the next two lines impossible).... One can no longer say that revolution is anarchy and disorder; it occurred in Havana because of treason, but that was not the case in Santiago de Cuba, which we can hold out as a model every time the Revolution is accused of anarchy and disorganization. It is well that people should know of the negotiations between General Cantillo and me. If the people are not too tired, I can tell you that after the agreements were made, when we had already suspended operations in Santiago de Cuba, since on the 28th our troops were quite near to the city and had completed all the preparatory work necessary for the attack on it, according to the interview we were to make a series of changes, abandoning the operation at Santiago de Cuba. Instead, we were to direct our troops elsewhere, in fact, to a place where it was believed that the Movement might not be victorious from the outset. Message From Cantillo When we had completed all our movements, the column which was to march on the capital received the following note from General Cantillo, just a few hours before it was due to leave. The text of the note read as

Fidel Castro Speaks

follows: "Circumstances have changed considerably and now are favorable to a national solution, in accordance with all desires for Cuba." Yet, the major factors could not be more favorable and every circumstance pointed to triumph. It was therefore strange that he should come and say that circumstances had changed greatly and favorably. The circumstances were that Batista and Tabernilla had agreed and the success of the coup was assured. I recommended that nothing should be done at the moment and that we should await the course of events over the next weeks, up to (January) 6th. Obviously, given the indefinitely prolonged truce while they were taking care of everything in Havana, my immediate reply was as follows: "The tenor of the note is entirely in contradiction with our agreements. Moreover, it is ambiguous and incomprehensible and has made me lose confidence in the seriousness of the agreements. Hostilities will break out tomorrow at 3 p.m., the date and time agreed upon for the launching of the movement." Something very curious happened immediately thereafter in addition to the receipt of the very short note. I advised the commanding officer at Santiago de Cuba, through the bearer of the

Fidel Castro Speaks

message, that if hostilities were to break out because the agreements were not fulfilled and we had to attack the first at Santiago de Cuba, they could do nothing other than surrender. We Demand the Surrender of Santiago de Cuba My phrase was that we demanded the surrender of the town if hostilities were to break out and if we were to initiate the attack. However, the bearer of the note did not interpret me correctly. He told Colonel Rego Rubido that I demanded the surrender of the town as a precondition to any agreement. He did not add that I had said, "in the event of our launching an attack." However, I had not said that I demanded the surrender of the town as a condition from General Cantillo. As a result of this message, the commanding officer at Santiago de Cuba sent me a very enigmatic and punctilious reply which I will read to you, indicating, naturally, that he felt very offended with what had been said to him in error. It read as follows: "The solution found is neither a coup d'état nor a military revolt and yet we believe that it is the most advisable solution for Dr. Fidel Castro, in accordance with his ideas and one which would place the destinies of the country in his hands within 48 hours. It is not a local but a national solution and any

Fidel Castro Speaks

indiscretion might compromise or destroy it, leading to chaos. Therefore, we hope you will have confidence in our decisions and you will receive the solution before the 6th. As for Santiago, owing to the note and to the words of the messenger, it will be necessary to change the plan and not enter the city." Arms Cannot Be Surrendered Without Honor His words caused a certain amount of bad feeling among the key personnel. It was argued that no arms would be surrendered without fighting, that arms are not surrendered, that arms are not surrendered to an ally, that arms cannot be surrendered without honor. All of which are very beautiful phrases when spoken by the commander of the garrison of Santiago de Cuba, if he has no confidence in us; or if Santiago de Cuba is attacked, they will regard it as equivalent to breaking the agreements, which will interrupt the negotiations for the solution offered, thereby formally absolving us from any compromise. It was our hope that, given the time required to act in one way or another, the reply would arrive in time to be sent to Havana by the Viscount flying out in the afternoon. My answer to Colonel Jose Rego Rubido's note was as follows: "In liberated Cuban Territory, 31 December 1958. Dear

Fidel Castro Speaks

Colonel, a regrettable error has occurred in the
transmission of my message to you, due
perhaps to the haste with which I replied to your
note. This is what I surmise from the
conversation I have since held with its bearer. I
did not tell him that the conditions we
established in the agreement entered into
encompassed the surrender of the garrison of
Santiago de Cuba to our forces. This showed a
lack of courtesy to our visitor and would have
constituted an unworthy and offensive proposal
to the military forces who so cordially sought us
out. The question was entirely different. An
agreement was reached and a plan adopted
between the leader of the military movement
and ourselves which was to go into effect as
from 3 p.m. on 31 December. The plan included
details established after careful analysis of the
problems to be faced, and was to begin with the
revolt of the garrison at Santiago de Cuba. I
persuaded General Cantillo of the advantages
to be derived from beginning at Oriente rather
than in Colombia because the mass of the
people greatly feared any coup starting in the
barracks in the Capital of the Republic, stressing
how difficult it would be, in that case, to insure
that the people joined up with the movement. He

Fidel Castro Speaks

stated that he was in full agreement with my viewpoint on the matter and was only concerned with maintaining order in the Capital, so we jointly agreed on measures necessary to avoid that danger. These measures involved the advance of our column toward Santiago de Cuba, to be exact. It was to be a combined effort of the military, the people and ourselves, a sort of revolutionary movement which, from the outset, would be backed by the confidence of the whole nation. According to what was established, we suspended the operations that were underway and undertook new displacements of our forces in other directions -- such as Holguin, where the presence of well-known figureheads practically insured resistance to the revolutionary military movement. When all our preparatory tasks were completed, I received yesterday's message, indicating that the plan of action agreed upon was not to be fulfilled." Apparently There Were Other Plans "Apparently there were other plans but I was not to be informed of them because, in fact, the matter was no longer in our hands. Therefore all we could do was wait because one party was changing everything. Our own forces were being endangered, although according to

Fidel Castro Speaks

our understanding and what was being said they were being sent off on difficult operations. And we remained subject to the outcome of the risks which General Cantillo took on his frequent trips to Havana. Militarily, these trips might well prove to be a disaster for us. You must realize that everything is very confused at this moment and Batista is an artful, crafty individual who knows only too well how to make the best use of a risk that can prove dangerous to others. All that can be asked is that we renounce all of the advantages gained during the past few weeks, and stand by, waiting patiently, for events to take their due course. I made it quite clear that it could not be an operation on the part of the military alone. We didn't have to undergo the horror of two years of war for this, and then stand with our arms crossed, doing nothing, at the most critical moment. They cannot expect this of men who have known no rest in the struggle against oppression. This cannot be done even though it is your intention to hand over the power to the revolutionaries. It is not power that is important to us, but that the Revolution should fulfill its destiny. I am even concerned by the fact that the military, through any unjustifiable excess of scruples, should

Fidel Castro Speaks

facilitate the flight of the principal criminals who would be able to escape abroad with their vast fortunes, and then from some foreign country do all the harm possible to our country. I Am Not Interested in Power "I should add that, personally, I am not interested in power nor do I envisage assuming it at any time. All that I will do is to make sure that the sacrifices of so many compatriots should not be in vain, whatever the future may hold in store for me. "In all my dealings, I have always acted loyally and frankly. One should never consider what has been obtained underhandedly and with duplicity as a triumph and the language of honor which you have heard from my lips is the only language I know. Never in the course of the meetings with General Cantillo did we refer to the word 'surrender.' what I said yesterday and what I repeat today is that, as of 3 p.m. of the 31st (December), the date and time agreed upon, we could not cut short the truce with Santiago de Cuba because that would have been exceedingly detrimental to the people. "Last night, the rumor circulated here that General Cantillo had been arrested in Havana and that various young men had been found murdered in the cemetery of Santiago de Cuba.

Fidel Castro Speaks

I had the feeling that we had been wasting our time most unhappily. And yet today, luckily enough, it seems certain that the General is at his post. What is the need for such risks? What I said to the messenger about surrender, and which was not communicated literally -- as would appear to have been confirmed by the terms of his note today -- was the following: that if hostilities were to break out because the terms of the agreement had not been fulfilled, we would be compelled t attack the garrison at Santiago de Cuba. This would be inevitable, since that was the objective of our efforts over the past few months. In this case, once the operation was under way, we would have to demand the surrender of those defending the garrison. This does not mean to imply that we think they will surrender without fighting because I know that even when there is not reason to fight, Cuban military forces will defend their positions adamantly and this has cost me many lives. "All I meant was that once the blood of our forces had been shed in the attempt to conquer a given objective, no other solution would be acceptable. Even though the cost be extremely heavy, in view of the present conditions of the forces defending the regime,

Fidel Castro Speaks

and since these forces cannot support the garrison of Santiago de Cuba, the latter must inevitably fall into our hands. Basic Objective of the Campaign "This was the basic objective of our whole campaign over the past two months and a plan of such scale cannot be held up for a week without giving rise to grave consequences, should the military movement fail. Moreover, it would mean losing the most opportune time -- which is the present -- when the dictatorship is suffering severe losses in the provinces of Oriente and Las Villas. We are faced with the dilemma of either waiving the advantages gained by our victory or exchanging an assured victory for one that is otherwise. Do you believe that in the face of yesterday's ambiguous and laconic note, containing a unilateral decision, I could hold myself responsible for delaying the plans? "As a military man, you must admit that too much is being asked of us. You have not stopped digging trenches for a single moment and you could well make use of those trenches against us... Some one like Pedraza, or Pilar Garcia or Canizares... and if General Cantillo is relieved of his command, and if his trusted lieutenants go with him, you cannot expect us to remain idle. You see, they have promised us the

Fidel Castro Speaks

absurd and although they defend themselves
valiantly with their arms, we have no alternative
but to attack, because we also have very sacred
commitments to fulfill. We desire that these
honorable military men be much more than
mere allies. We want them to be our
companions in a single cause, the cause of
Cuba. Above all, I wish you, yourself, my friend,
not to misinterpret my attitude. Do not believe
that I am being overly rigid as regards the
tactics involving the holding off of an attack in
the Santiago de Cuba area. In order that no
possible doubt whatever may persist, I will
confirm that although at any time before the
fighting begins we can renew our negotiations,
as of today it must be made clear that the attack
will take place momentarily and that nothing will
convince us to alter the plans again." A Letter
from Colonel Rego Colonel Rego replied in a
very punctilious note, worthy of the greatest
praise, which reads as follows: "Sir, I beg to
acknowledge receipt of your letter of today's
date, and believe me, I wish to thank you most
sincerely for the explanation regarding the
previous message. However, I must confess
that I felt some error of interpretation was
involved since I have observed your line of

Fidel Castro Speaks

conduct for some time and know that you are a man of principle. I ignored the details of the original plan because I was only informed of the first part of it. I might add that I am also not aware of some of the details of the present plan. I believe you are partly right in your analysis of the first part of the original plan. However, I believe that a few more days would be necessary before it could be consummated and we would never be able to prevent some of the major, intermediary and minor guilty parties from escaping. I am among those who believe it is absolutely essential to give an example of Cuba of all those who take advantage of the positions of power they occupy to commit every possible type of punishable offense. Unfortunately, history is plagued with a series of similar cases ad rarely do the criminals fall into the hands of the competent authorities. "I am fully aware of your concern for the men who have the least responsibility for the course of historical events." Opposed to the Flight of the Guilty "I have no reason whatsoever to believe that any person is attempting to facilitate the escape of the guilty, and, personally, I might add that I am opposed to their flight." That was Colonel Rego Rubido's view. However, he also added that should such

Fidel Castro Speaks

an event take place, the historical responsibility for such an act would fall on the shoulders of those who facilitated the escape, and never on those of anyone else. "I believe," he said, "that everything will take place in accordance with your ideas, and that it will be for the good of Cuba and of the Revolution of which you are the leader. I heard of a young student who had been murdered and whose body was in the cemetery. Today, I myself made sure that every possible measure be taken to determine who was guilty of those crimes and what the circumstances of his death were, and how it took place, just as I had done a few days ago, not sparing any effort until I am able to put the suspected authors of this crime at the disposal of the competent authorities. Lastly, I should advise you that I sent a message through to the General, letting him know that I had obtained a plane to carry your note to him. Do not be impatient for I feel sure that even before the date established as the maximum limit you will be in Havana. When the General left here, I asked him to let me have the helicopter and a pilot, just in case you might like to fly over Santiago de Cuba on Sunday afternoon. "With sincerest greetings and my warmest wishes for

Fidel Castro Speaks

a Happy New Year, (Signed) Colonel Rego
Rubido." Surprised by the Coup in Colombia
This was the state of our negotiations when
Colonel Rego, Commander of the garrison of
Santiago de Cuba and I were equally surprised
by the coup d'etat in Colombia, which was
completely in contradiction with all that had
been agreed upon. The first thing done and the
most criminal aspect of all was that Batista was
allowed to escape, and with him Tabernilla, and
the other major criminals. They allowed them to
escape with their millions of pesos; yes, they
allowed them to flee with the three or four
hundred million pesos they had stolen. This will
prove very costly for us because now, from
Santo Domingo and from other countries, they
will be directing propaganda against the
Revolution, plotting all the harm they can
against our cause and for a good many years
we will have them there, threatening our people,
and causing the people to remain in a constant
state of alarm because they will be conspiring
against us and paying others to do so also.
What did we do as soon as we learned of the
blow? We heard about it on Radio Progreso and
by that time, guessing what their plans were, as
I was making a statement I was told that Batista

Fidel Castro Speaks

had left for Santo Domingo. Is it a rumor? I wondered. Could it be a trick? I sent someone out to confirm the story and was informed that Batista and Tabernilla had actually gone to Santo Domingo. And the most astonishing thing of all was that General Cantillo declared that this movement had taken place thanks to the patriotic intentions of General Batista, who had resigned in order to avoid bloodshed. What do you think about that? There is something else I must tell you in order to let you see what kind of a coup had been prepared. Pedraza had been appointed to membership of the Junta and then he left. I don't think one need add anything else to explain the nature of the aims of those responsible for carrying out the coup. Subsequently, they did not appoint Urrutia to the Presidency, that is, the man proclaimed by the movement and by all the revolutionary organizations. The person they chose is no less than the oldest member of the Supreme Court bench, and all his colleagues are quite old themselves. And above all he is a man who has been a President up to the present time: a President of a Supreme Court of Justice which never dispenses any justice, which never did dispense any justice whatsoever. It Appears To

Fidel Castro Speaks

Be Only Half a Revolution What would the result of all this be? Only half a revolution. A compromise, a caricature of a revolution. Mr. Jack Straw, or whatever name you may wish to give this Mr. Piedra who, if he has not resigned by now should be getting ready to do so, because we are going to make him resign in Havana. I do not believe he will last twenty-four hours in office. It will break all records. They appoint this gentleman and, isn't it perfect, Cantillo becomes a national hero, the defender of Cuba's freedoms, the Lord and Master of Cuba, and there is Mr. Piedra... It would simply mean getting rid of one dictator to put another in his place. Every order contained in the documents referring to the movement in Colombia indicated that it was to be a counterrevolutionary uprising. In all the orders, the general trend was away from the aims of the people, and in all the orders there was an atmosphere of something suspect. Mr. Piedra immediately made an appeal, or stated that he was going to make an appeal to the rebels and to a peace commission. Meanwhile, we were supposed to be so calm and trusting; we would put down our guns and abandon everything and go and plead and pay homage to Mr. Piedra and

Fidel Castro Speaks

Mr. Cantillo. Cantillo and Piedra Out of Touch With Reality It is obvious that both Cantillo and Piedra were out of touch with reality because I believe that the Cuban people have learned a great deal and we rebels have also learned something. That was the situation this morning but it is not the situation this evening, because many things have changed. Given these facts, given this betrayal, I ordered all the rebel commanders to continue marching on toward their targets, and in keeping with this, I also immediately ordered all the columns allocated to the Santiago de Cuba operations to advance against that garrison. I want you to know that our forces were firmly determined to take Santiago de Cuba by assault. This would have been regrettable because it would have led to much bloodshed and tonight would not have been a night of celebration and happiness, as it is, it would not have been a night of peace and fraternization, as it is. I must acknowledge that if there was not a bloody battle waged here in Santiago de Cuba, it is due largely to the patriotic attitude of Army Colonel Jose Rego Rubido, to the commanders of the frigates Maximo Gomez and Maceo and to the chief of the Santiago de Cuba Naval District, as well as

Fidel Castro Speaks

to the officer who was acting as Chief of Police. Avoiding a Bloody Battle Citizens, it is only just that we should recognize these facts here and now and be thankful to the men responsible for them. They contributed to averting considerable bloodshed and to converting this morning's counterrevolutionary movement into the revolutionary movement of this afternoon. We had no alternative other than to attack because we could not allow the Colombia coup to be consolidated. Therefore, it was necessary to attack. When the troops were already marching out against their targets, Colonel Rego made use of a helicopter to try and locate me. The Navy commanders contacted us and placed themselves unconditionally at the service of the Revolution. Backed by the support of their two vessels, equipped with heavy firing capacity, and by the Naval District and the Police, I called a meeting of all the Army officers stationed at the Santiago de Cuba garrison -- and there are over a hundred of these officers. I explained to them that I was not the least worried by the thought of addressing them because I knew I was right, and I knew they would understand my arguments and that we would reach an agreement in the course of the meeting. Indeed,

Fidel Castro Speaks

in the early evening, just at nightfall, I went to
the meeting at the Escande which was attended
by nearly all the Army officers in Santiago de
Cuba. Many of them were young men who were
clearly anxious to struggle and fight for the good
of their country. I met with these military men
and spoke to them of our aims for our country,
of what we wanted for the country, of the
manner in which we had always dealt with the
military and of all the harm done to the army by
the tyrants. I said I did not think it fair that all
military men be regarded equally, that the
criminals were only a small minority, that there
were many honorable men in the army who I
knew repudiated criminal tactics, abuse and
injustice. I knew it was not easy for the military
to develop a specific type of action. There Was
Great Fear in the Army It was clear that when
the highest positions in the army were in the
hands of the Tabernilla and the Pilar Garcia,
relatives and unconditional supporters of
Batista, there was a generalized feel of great
fear in the Army. One could not ask an officer
individually to accept any responsibility. There
were two kinds of military men and we know
them well. There were military men like Sosa
Blanco, Canizares, Sanchez Mosquera and

Fidel Castro Speaks

Chaviano, known for their crimes and the cowardly murder of unfortunate peasants; and then there are military men who have waged honorable campaigns, who never murdered anyone, nor burned down houses, men such as Commander Quevedo, who was our prisoner after his heroic resistance at the Battle of Jibo and who is still an Army officer. Men like Commander Sierra and many other officers who never in their lives burned down a house. However, this type of officer got no promotion. Those who were promoted were the criminals because Batista always made a point of recompensing crime. Support for the Cuban Revolution For example, we have the case of Colonel Rego Rubido who does not owe his position to the dictatorship since he was already a Colonel when the 10 March coup took place. The fact is that I was given the support of the Army officers in Santiago de Cuba and the army officers in Santiago de Cuba gave their unconditional backing to the Cuban Revolution. When the Navy, Army and Police officers met together, they agreed to condemn the Colombia uprising and to support the Legal Government of the Republic because it has the backing of the majority of the population, and is represented by

Fidel Castro Speaks

Dr. Manuel Urrutia Lleo, and they also agreed to support the Cuban Revolution. Thanks to their attitude, we were able to prevent much bloodshed; thanks to their attitude, this afternoon we saw the birth of a truly revolutionary movement. I quite understand that among the people there may be many justifiably passionate feelings. I appreciate the concern for justice evinced by our people and I promise to give them justice, but I want to ask the people, above all and before all else, to remain calm. Before All Else, Power Must Be Consolidated At the present moment, power must be consolidated before we do anything else. Before all else, power must be consolidated. After that, we will appoint a commission, made up of reputable military men and officers of the Rebel Army to take the necessary measures. These will include establishing responsibilities where they are due. No one will oppose such measures because it is precisely the army and the armed forces who are most concerned in insuring that the guilt of a few should not be borne by the whole corps. They are the ones most interested in insuring that the wearing of a uniform not be regarded as degrading, and that the guilty be punished in order that the innocent

Fidel Castro Speaks

not be charged with the disreputable acts of others. We would ask the people to have confidence in us because we know how to fulfill our obligations. Those were the circumstances surrounding the meeting held this afternoon -- a meeting that proved to be a truly revolutionary movement in which the people, the military and the rebels participated. The Entry into Santiago de Cuba Words fail us to describe the enthusiasm of the military in Santiago de Cuba. As a proof of their trust, I asked the military to join me in entering Santiago de Cuba, so that here I am with all the Army officers. There are the tanks that are at the service of the Revolution. there is the artillery and the service of the Revolution. And there are the vessels, now at the service of the Revolution. And finally the people. The people who at the outset... I need not add that the Revolution can depend on the people because this is a well-known fact. However, the people, who at the outset had only shotguns, now have artillery, tanks and well-armed vessels, and many trained army technicians to help us handle them. Now the people are properly armed. And let me assure you that if when we were only 12 men, we never lost faith, now that we have 12 tanks there, how

Fidel Castro Speaks

are we going to lose faith? Let me tell you that today, tonight, as of this dawn -- because daybreak is at hand, the eminent magistrate Dr. Manuel Urrutia Lleo will take over the presidency of the Republic. Does Dr. Urrutia have the support of the people or does he not have the support of the people? What I really mean to say is that it is the President of the Republic, the legal president, who has the support of the people of Cuba and that is Dr. Manuel Urrutia. Who wants Mr. Piedra as President? Then if no one wants Mr. Piedra as President, how are they going to impose Mr. Piedra on us now? March toward the Capital Since those are the instructions given by the people of Santiago de Cuba, and since they represent the feelings of all the people of all Cuba, as soon as this meeting is over I will march with the veteran troops of Sierra Maestra, with the tanks and the artillery, toward the Capital in order to fulfill the will of people. We are here entirely at the request of the people. The mandate of the people is the only legal mandate at present. The President is elected by the people and not by a council in Colombia, meeting at four o'clock in the morning. The people have elected their President and this

Fidel Castro Speaks

means that from this moment on the most powerful legal authority in the Republic has been established. Not a single one, not a single one of the appointments and promotions made by the Military Junta in the early hours of today is at all valid. All the appointments and promotions in the Army are annulled, all the appointments and promotions, I mean, that were made at dawn today. Anyone accepting a commission from the treacherous Junta which met this morning is regarded as adopting a counterrevolutionary attitude, call it by whatever name you wish, and as a result will be branded as an outlaw. I am absolutely convinced that by tomorrow morning all the army commands throughout the country will have accepted the decisions taken by the President of the Republic. The President will immediately appoint the chiefs of the Army, the Navy and the Police. Because of the very valuable service rendered now to the Revolution and because he placed his thousands of men at the service of the Revolution, we would recommend that colonel Rego Rubido be made Chief of the Army. Similarly, the Chief of the Navy will be one of the two commanders who first placed their vessels at the orders of the Revolution.

Fidel Castro Speaks

And I would recommend to the President of the Republic that Commander Efigenio Almejeiras be appointed national Chief of Police. He lost three brothers in the Revolution, was one of the members of the gamma expeditionary force and one of the most able men in the revolutionary army. Almejeiras is on duty in the Guantanamo operations but will arrive here tomorrow. Things Will Be the Way the People Want Them All I can do is ask you to give us time and to allow time to the civil powers of the Republic, so that we can do things the way the people want them; but they must be done gradually, little by little. I would only ask one thing of the people, and that is that you remain calm. (A voice is heard shouting Oriente Federal!) No... no, the Republic, above all else, must remain united. What you must demand is justice for Oriente (province). Time is a highly important factor in all things. The Revolution cannot be completed in a single day but you may be sure that we will carry the Revolution through to the full. You may be sure that for the first time the Republic will be truly and entirely free and the people will have their just recompense. Power was not achieved through politics, but through the sacrifices of hundreds and thousands of our fellows. It is not

Fidel Castro Speaks

a promise we make to ourselves but to the people, the whole Cuban nation; the man who has taken over power has no commitments with anyone other than with the people. Che Guevara has been ordered to march on the Capital, not on the provisional Capital of the Republic. Commander Camilo Cienfuegos of Number 2 Column -- the Antonio Maceo column -- was likewise ordered to march on Havana and to take over command of the Colombia military camp. The orders issued by the President of the Republic were carried out, as is required by the mandate of the Revolution. We must not be blamed for the excesses occurring in Havana. General Cantillo and his fellow-conspirators of this day's dawn are to blame for those. They believed that they could overcome the situation there. In Santiago de Cuba, where a genuine revolution took place, complete order has reigned. In Santiago de Cuba, the people joined with the military and the revolutionaries in a way I cannot describe. The head of the Government, the head of the Army and the head of the Navy will be in Santiago de Cuba and their orders must be obeyed by every authority in the country. It is our hope that every honorable military man will respect these instructions.

Fidel Castro Speaks

There Is No Need to Fear the Revolution It is important to remember that primarily the military forces are at the service of law and of authority, not improperly constituted authorities but the legitimate authority. No reputable Army man need fear anything from the Revolution. In this struggle, there are no conquered ones because the only conqueror is the people. There are men who have fallen on one side and the other, but we have all joined together that the victory may be the nation's. We have all joined together, the reputable military and the revolutionaries. There will be no more bloodshed. I hope that no group puts up any resistance because apart from such an attitude proving foolhardy, it would be overcome in short shift. Moreover, it would be resistance against the Law, against the Republic and against the feelings of the whole Cuban nation. It was necessary to organize today's movement in order to prevent another war taking place in six months' time. What happened at the time of Machado's coup? Well one of machado's generals also organized a coup d'etat, removed Machado from power and put in a new President who remained in office for 15 days. Then the sergeants came along and said those officers were responsible for Machado's

Fidel Castro Speaks

dictatorship and that they could not countenance them. The revolutionary spirit spread and the officers were ousted. That cannot take place now. those officers have the backing of the people and of the troops. They also enjoy the prestige acquired by having joined a truly revolutionary movement. The people will respect and esteem these officers and it will not be necessary for them to use force nor to go about the streets armed nor to attempt to strike fear in the hearts of the people. Order, Freedom and Justice True order is that based on freedom, on respect and on justice, but at the same time that which precludes the use of force. Henceforward, the people shall be entirely free and the people know how to conduct themselves, as they have proven today. We have achieved the peace that our country needs. Santiago de Cuba has paid for its freedom without bloodshed. That is why happiness reigns supreme here. That is why the military, today, condemned and repudiated the Colombia coup, in order to join the revolution unconditionally. Therefore, they deserve our acknowledgment of their motivation, our thanks and our respect. In the future, the armed forces of the Republic will be regarded as exemplary,

Fidel Castro Speaks

given their ability, their training and the manner in which they identified with the cause of the people and because, henceforward, their rifles will be solely and always at the service of the people. There will be no more coups d'etat, no more war, because we have now taken care to prevent a repetition of what happened to Machado. To make the present case -- the one that took place at dawn today -- resemble Machado's fall even more closely, those gentlemen put a Carlos Manuel in office, just as a Carlos Manuel had been put in office previously. What we will not have this time is a Batista because there will be no need for a 4 September which destroys the discipline in the Armed Forces. It will be remembered that it was Batista who was responsible for the armed uprising at that time. His policy consisted in cajoling the soldiers in order to disguise the authority of the officers. The officers will have authority; there will be discipline in the Army; there will be a military penal code, in which any violation of human rights, any dishonorable or immoral acts by any military personnel, will be severely punished. There will be no privileges; there will be no privileges for anyone; and the members of the Armed Forces who are capable

Fidel Castro Speaks

and deserving will be promoted. It will not be as it has been in the past -- that is, that relations and friends are promoted, regardless of grades. This sort of thing will finish for the military as it will finish for laborers. There will be no more exploitation or compulsory contributions, which for the workers represent the trade union payments and for the military represent a peso here for the First Lady and two pesos elsewhere for something else and so all their pay dwindles away. Honesty in Respect of What is Collected Naturally, the whole population can expect it of us and can count on it. However, I have spoken of the military so that they will know that they can also count on the Revolution for all the improvements which have been lacking until now, because if the budgetary resources are not stolen, the military will be in a much better position than at the present. Moreover, the soldier will not be called upon to exercise the duty of a policeman because he will be busy with his own training in the barracks; the soldier will not be engaged in police work but will be busy being a soldier. We will not have to resort to short-wave systems. I think that I should add that we rebels make use of short-wave facilities because this is advisable. However, the short-

Fidel Castro Speaks

wave facilities have not made reference to assassins, have not involved sudden stopping of cars in front of houses nor ambushes at midnight. I am certain that as soon as the President of the Republic takes office and assumes command of the situation, he will decree the re-establishment of all rights and freedoms, including the absolute freedom of the press, of all individual rights, of all trade union rights, and of the rights and demands of the rural workers and our own free people. We will not forget our peasants in the Sierra Maestra and those in the interior of the country. I will not go and live in Havana because I want to live in Sierra Maestra, at least in that part for which I feel a very deep sense of gratitude. I will never forget those country people and as soon as I have a free moment we will see about building the first school city with seats for 20,000 children. We will do it with the help of the people and the rebels will work with them there. We will ask each citizen for a bag of cement and a trowel. I know we will have the help of our industry and of business and we will not forget any of the sectors of our population. Re-Establishment of the Economy The country's economy will be re-established immediately.

Fidel Castro Speaks

This year it is we who will take care of the sugar cane to prevent its being burnt, because this year the tax on sugar is not going to be used for the purchase of murderous weapons nor for planes and bombs with which to attack the people. We will take care of communications and already from Jiguani to Palma Soriano the telephone lines have been re-established, and the railroad is being rebuilt. There will be a harvest all over the country and there will be good wages because I know that this is the intention of the President of the Republic. There will be good prices because the fear that there would be no harvest has raised prices on the world market. The peasants can sell their coffee and the cattle breeders can sell their fat steers in Havana because fortunately we triumphed soon enough to prevent their being ruins of any kind. It is not my place to say all these things. You know that we keep our word, and what we promise we fulfill and we promise less than what we intend to fulfill; we promise not more but less and we intend to do more than we have offered the people of Cuba. We do not believe that all the problems can be solved readily; we know the road is sown with obstacles, but we are men of good faith and we are always ready to face

Fidel Castro Speaks

great difficulties. The people can be certain of one thing, and that is that we may make one or even many mistakes. But the only thing which cannot be said of us is that we have stolen, that we have profited from our position, that we have betrayed the movement. I know that the people can forgive mistakes but not dishonorable deeds, and what we had here were dishonorable men. In accepting the presidency, Dr. Manuel Urrutia, from the very first moment when he was invested in office, from the moment when he swore his oath before the people as President of the Republic, became the maximum authority in the country. Let no one think that I intend to exercise any power greater than that of the President of the Republic. I will be the first to obey orders issued by the civilian authority of the Republic and I will be the first to set an example. We will carry out his orders and within the scope of the authority granted to us we will try to do the utmost for our people without any personal ambition, because fortunately we are immune to the temptations of such ambitions and such vanity. What greater glory could we have than the affection of our people? What greater reward could we envision than the thousands of arms waving before us,

Fidel Castro Speaks

full of hope, and faith in us and affection for us.
We shall never allow ourselves to be influenced
by vanity or ambition because, in the words of
the Apostle, all the glory of the world can be
contained within a single ear of corn, and there
is no greater reward or satisfaction than to fulfill
one's duty as we have been doing until the
present time and as we shall always continue to
do. In saying this, I am not speaking in my own
name but in the name of the thousands and
thousands of combatants who ensured the
victory of the people. I speak on behalf of our
deep sentiments and of our devotion for our
people. I have in mind the respect we owe to
our dead, to the fallen, who shall not be
forgotten and whose faithful companions we
shall always be. This time they shall not say of
us as has been said of others in the past that we
betrayed the memory of those who died
because the years will still be given by those
who died. Frank Pais is not physically among
us, nor are many others, but they are all
spiritually present and the mere knowledge that
their sacrifice was not in vain recompenses us in
part for the immense emptiness which they left
behind them. We Shall Be Generous to
Everyone Fresh flowers will continue to adorn

Fidel Castro Speaks

their tombstones; their children shall not be forgotten because assistance will be given to the families of the fallen. We rebels will not ask for retroactive pay over the years during which we struggled because we feel proud not to be paid for the services rendered to Cuba. Indeed, it is quite possible that we should continue to fulfill our obligations without asking for pay because this is immaterial if funds are lacking. What exists is goodwill and we shall do everything necessary. However, I will repeat here what I have already said, "and history will absolve me," that we shall insure that maintenance, assistance, and education shall not be lacking for the children of the military who died fighting against us because they are not to blame for the errors of the tyrant. We shall be generous to everyone because, as I have said before, here there are no vanquished, but only victors. The war criminals will all be punished because it is the irrevocable duty of the Revolution to do so and the people can be certain that we shall fulfill that duty. The people should also be sure that when justice reigns there will be no revenge because if on the morrow there are to be no assaults made against anyone, justice must reign now. Since

Fidel Castro Speaks

there will be justice, there will be no revenge nor will there be hatred. Let Trujillo Not Make Any Mistake We shall exile hatred from the Republic, that hatred which is a damned and evil shadow bequeathed to us by ambition and tyranny. The pity is that the major criminals should have escaped. There are thousands of men who would pursue them, but we must respect the laws of other countries. It would be easy for us because we have more than enough volunteers to pursue those delinquents, ready and willing to risk their lives. However, we do not wish to give the appearance of a people who violate the laws of other peoples; we shall respect these laws while ours are respected. notwithstanding, I will issue one warning and that is that if in Santo Domingo they begin to conspire against the Revolution, if Trujillo... makes any mistake and directs any aggression against us, it will be a sorry day for him. (At one time I said that Trijillo had harmed Batista by selling him arms and the harm he did us not so much in selling arms but in selling weapons of poor quality, so bad, in fact, that when they fell into our hands they were no use at all.) However, he did sell bombs and those served to murder many peasants. We have no wish to return the rifles because they

Fidel Castro Speaks

are worth nothing, but we would like to reciprocate with something better. In the first place, it is logical that the political refugees from Santo Domingo should have their safest asylum and most comfortable home here and that the political refugees of every dictatorship should find here their best protection, since we, too, have been refugees. The Rejoicing in Latin America If Santo Domingo is to be converted into an arsenal of counterrevolutionaries, if Santo Domingo is to be a base for conspiracies against the Cuban Revolution and if these gentlemen devote themselves to conspiracies over there, it would be better for them to leave Santo Domingo immediately. We say this, because they will not be very safe there either and it will not be because of us since we have no right to intervene in the problems of Santo Domingo. It will be because the citizens of the Dominican Republic have learnt from Cuba's example and conditions will be very grave indeed there. The citizens of the Dominican Republic have learned that one can struggle against tyranny and defeat and this is the lesson dictatorships fear the most. Yet, it is a lesson which is encouraging for the Americas; a lesson exemplified just now in our country. All of

Fidel Castro Speaks

America is watching the course of the fate of this revolution. All the Americas are watching us and they follow our actions with their best wishes for our triumph as they will all of them support us in our times of need. Therefore, everything is joyful now, not only in Cuba but also in the Americas. They rejoice as we have rejoiced when a dictator has fallen in Latin America, so now they rejoice with the Cuban people. It is assumed that there will be justice, as I was saying, despite the enormous accumulation of sentiments and ideas stemming from the general disorder, commotion, and feelings registered in our minds today. As I was saying, it was a pity that the major criminals escaped. We now know who was responsible because the people know who is to blame for their escape as they know that they also left here not the most unfortunate but the dullest, those who were penniless, the rank and file who took their orders from the major criminals. They allowed the major criminals to escape so that the people might state their anger and their indignation upon those who were least to blame although it is only right that they should be justly punished in order to learn their lesson. The same thing always happens, the people tell this

Fidel Castro Speaks

group that the "big shots" will get away and they will be left behind and, nevertheless, though some of them may leave, others remain and must be punished. The top men may go but they will also have their punishment, a harsh punishment, for it is harsh to be exiled from one's country for the rest of one's days because they will, even in the best of circumstances, be ostracized for the rest of their lives as criminals and thieves who fled precipitately. Both a Common and a Political Delinquent Criminal If only one could see Mr. Batista now -- through the eye of a needle, as the people say. If only one could see the proud, handsome Mr. Batista, who never made a single speech but that he described others as cowards, wretched villains, etcetera. Here, we have not even used the epithet of "villain" for anyone. Here we do not breathe hatred, nor are we proud or disdainful as are those who made speeches during the dictatorship. Like that man who claimed that he had a single bullet in his pistol when he entered Colombia and who left in the early hours of the dawn, on a plane, with a single bullet in his pistol. And it was proved that dictators are not so frightening nor so likely to commit suicide, because when they have lost the game, they

Fidel Castro Speaks

immediately take flight like cowards. The sad part of it is that they escaped when they could have been taken prisoners and had we caught Batista, we could have taken the 200 million from him. But we will claim the money, wherever he is hiding it, because they are not political delinquents but common criminals. And we will see those who turn up in the embassies, if Mr. Cantillo has not already given them safe-conducts. We will distinguish then between the political prisoners but nothing for the common criminals. They will have to go before the courts and prove that they are political delinquents. However, if it should be proved that they are common criminals, they will have to appear before the proper authorities. For instance, Mujal, as big and as fat as he is, nobody knows where he is hiding at the present time. I can't understand how they got away. Nevertheless you will remember these unfortunate wretches.... They May Speak Freely, Whether For or Against At last the people have been able to free themselves from this rabble. Now anyone may speak out, whether they are for or against. But anyone who wishes to do so may speak out. That was not the case here previously because until the present time, they were the only ones

Fidel Castro Speaks

(allowed) to speak out; only they spoke out. And they spoke against us. There will be freedom for those who speak in our favor and for those who speak against us and criticize us. There will be freedom for all men because we have achieved freedom for all men. We shall never feel offended; we shall always defend ourselves and we shall follow a single precept, that of respect for the rights and feelings of others. Other names have been mentioned here. Those people! Heaven alone knows in what embassy, on what beach, in what boat they now find themselves. We were able to get rid of them. If they have a tiny shack, or a small boat, or a tiny farm somewhere round here, we will naturally have to confiscate it, because we must sound the warning that the employees of tyranny, the representatives, the senators, etcetera, those who did not necessarily steal but who accepted their remuneration, will have to pay back, up to the last penny, what they received over these four years, because they received it illegally. The will have to pay back to the Republic the money they received as remuneration and if they do not reimburse the national coffers, we will confiscate whatever property they have. That is quite apart from what they may have stolen. Those who robbed will not be allowed to retain any of the stolen goods. That is the law of the Revolution. It is not fair to send a man to prison for stealing a chicken or a turkey, and at the same time allow those who stole millions of pesos to spend a delightful life wandering around. Triumph Without Obligations Let the thieves of yesterday and today beware! Let them beware! Because the Revolution's laws may reach out to draw in the guilty of every period. Because the Revolution has triumphed and has no obligations to anyone whatsoever. It's only obligation is to the people, to whom it owes its victory. I want to conclude for today. Remember that I must leave right away. It is my duty. What is more, you have been standing there for a good many hours. However, I see so many red and black flags on the dresses of our women followers that it is really hard for us to leave this platform, on which all of us here have felt the great emotion in all our lives. We would not do less than remember Santiago de Cuba with the greatest warmth. The few times we have met here -- a meeting on the Alameda and another on Trocha Avenue, at which I said that if we were deprived of our rights by force, we would recover them with our rifles in hand, and

Fidel Castro Speaks

yet they attributed the statement to Luis
Orlando. I kept quiet and at the time, while the
newspapers made it seem as if Luis Orlando
was the one who had done the most, although it
was I who did the most. Yet I was not very sure
whether or not things were well done because at
that time there was and the result was that we
had to exchange everything, the books and the
diagrams for rifles, while the peasants
exchanged their farm implements for rifles and
we all had to exchange everything for rifles.
Fortunately the task that required rifles is done;
so let us keep the rifles where they are, far away
from their eyes, because they will have to
defend our sovereignty and our rights. Yet,
when our people are threatened, it will not be
only the thirty or forty thousand armed men who
will fight, but the three or four or five hundred
thousand Cubans, men and women, who can
come here for their arms. There will be arms for
all those who wish to fight when the time comes
to defend our freedom. It has been proven that it
is not only the men who fight but that in Cuba
the women also fight. The best evidence of this
is the Mariana Grajales platoon, which made
such an outstanding showing in numerous
encounters. The women are as good soldiers as

Fidel Castro Speaks

our best military men and I wanted to prove that women can be good soldiers. The Work of the Women Soldiers At the outset, this scheme gave me a lot of trouble because they were very prejudiced. There were men who asked how on earth one could give a rifle to a woman while there was still a man alive to carry one. Yet on our front, women must be rescued because they are still the victims of discrimination insofar as labor is concerned and in other aspects of their lives. So we organized the women's units and these proved that women could fight, and when the men fight in a village and the women can fight alongside them, such villages are impregnable and the women of such villages cannot be defeated. We have organized the feminine combatants or militias and we will keep them trained -- all of them on a voluntary basis -- all these young women I see here with their black and red dresses recalled 26 July. And I ask all of you to learn to handle firearms. A People Is Aroused My dear Compatriots, this Revolution carried out with such sacrifice, our Revolution, the Revolution of the people, is now a magnificent and indestructible reality, a cause for no uncertain nor unjustified pride and a cause for the great joy that Cuba awaited. I

Fidel Castro Speaks

know that it is not only here in Santiago de Cuba, it is everywhere, from Punta de Maisi to Cape San Antonio. I long to see our people all along our route to the Capital, because I know I will encounter the same hopes, the same faith, a single people, aroused, a people who patiently bore all the sacrifices, who cared little for hunger, who when we gave them three days' leave for the re-establishment of communications, in order not to suffer hunger, the whole mass of the people protested because what they wanted was victory at any price. Such a people deserves a better fate, and deserves to achieve the happiness it has not had in 56 years of a Republican form of government. It deserves to become one of the leading nations in the world by reasons of its intelligence, its valor and the firmness of its decision. No one can allege that I am speaking as a demagogue. No one can charge that I am seeking to assuage the people. I have given ample proof of my faith in the people because when I landed with 82 men on the beaches of Cuba and people said we were mad, and asked us why we thought we could win the war, we replied, "Because we have the people behind us!" And when we were defeated for the first

Fidel Castro Speaks

time, and only a handful of men were left and yet we persisted in the struggle, we knew that this would be the outcome because we had faith in the people. When they dispersed us five times in forty-five days and we met up together again and renewed the struggle, it was because we had faith in the people. Today is the most palpable demonstration of the fact that our faith was justified. I have the greatest satisfaction in the knowledge that I believed so deeply in the people of Cuba and in having inspired my companions with this same faith. This faith is more than faith. It is complete security. This same faith that we have in you is the faith we wish you to have in us always. The Dream of the Founders The Republic was not freed in '95 and the dream was frustrated at the last minute. The Revolution did not take place in '33 and was frustrated by its enemies. However, this time the Revolution is backed by the mass of the people, and has all the revolutionaries behind it. It also has those who are honorable among the military. It is so vast and so uncontainable in its strength that this time its triumph is assured. We can say -- and it is with joy that we do so -- that in the four centuries since our country was founded, this will be the

Fidel Castro Speaks

first time that we are entirely free and that the work of the first settlers will have been completed. A few days ago, I could not resist the temptation to go and visit my Mother whom I had not seen for several years. On my return, as I was traveling along the road that cuts through Mangos de Baragua, late at night, the feelings of deep devotion, on the part of those of us who were riding in that vehicle, made us stop at the monument raised to the memory of those involved in the protest at Baragua and the beginning of the Invasion. At that late hour, there was only our presence in that place, the thought of the daring feats connected with our wars of independence, the idea that these men fought for 30 years and in the end did not see their dream come true, but witnessed only one more frustration of the Republic. Yet they had a presentiment that very soon the Revolution of which they dreamed, the mother country of which they dreamed, would be transformed into reality, and this gave us one of the greatest emotions possible. In my mind's eye, I saw these men relive their sacrifice, sacrifices which we also underwent. I conjured up their dreams and their aspirations, which were the same as our dreams and our aspirations and I ventured

Fidel Castro Speaks

to think that the present generation in Cuba
must render and has rendered homage,
gratitude and loyalty, as well as fervent tribute to
the heroes of our independence. In the Hands of
the Civil Authorities The men who fell in our
three wars of independence now join their
efforts to those of the men who fell in this war,
and of all those who fell in the struggle for
freedom. We can tell them that their dreams are
about to be fulfilled and that the time has finally
come when you, our people, our noble people,
our people who are so enthusiastic and have so
much faith, our people who demand nothing in
return for their affection, who demand nothing in
return for their confidence, who reward men with
a kindness far beyond anything they might
deserve, the time has come, I say, when you will
have everything you need. There is nothing left
for me to add, except, with modesty and
sincerity to say, with the deepest emotion, that
you will always have in us, in the fighters of the
Revolution, loyal servants whose sole motto is
service to you. On this date, today, when Dr.
Urrutia took over the Presidency of the Republic
Dr. Urrutia, the leader who declared that this
was a just Revolution -- on territory that has
been liberated, which by now is the whole of our

Fidel Castro Speaks

country, I declare that I will assume only those duties assigned to me, by him. The full authority of the Republic is vested in him. And our arms bow respectfully to the civil powers of the Civilian Republic of Cuba. All I have to say is that we hope that he will fulfill his duty because we naturally feel assured that he will know how to fulfill his duty. I surrender my authority to the Provisional President of the Republic of Cuba and with it I surrender to him the right to address the people of Cuba.

Fidel Castro on Counter-Revolutionaries

"You can be sure that we would not only have captured the weapons and the planes, but we would also have captured all the war criminals. We would have captured the legion; the army of Trujillo, and even Trujillo, right here." He continued that it was his feeling that the people had to be informed, and, "therefore, we had to be satisfied with what could be achieved during the week which began with the arrests of the plotters and ended yesterday when the arms-laden plane with 10 crew members fell into our hands at the Trinidad airport." After declaring that the counterrevolutionary conspiracy began soon after the fall of the Batista regime, Premier

Fidel Castro Speaks

Castro said that any successful revolution, like the Cuban revolution, was always opposed by certain interests. The elements that fled Cuba landed into Santo Domingo, he said. After pointing out that the Dominican Government had refused to return four Cuban planes, he stressed that Trujillo hated "not only the revolutionary government, but the country." Dr. Castro then declared that "from the first moment Trujillo began to maneuver and plot against us." After noting that Trujillo either "buy" or "murders" his enemies, Premier Castro declared that Trujillo did not limit himself to contacting Batista elements, but invited Commander William Morgan of the second front of Escambray into the plot, as well as Commanders Menoyo and Carrera. These men, he said, reported the proposal to the high command, which ordered them to accept. Castro said that in those days there were several groups, including the Rosa Blanca group, which were beginning to mobilize against the revolution, and that Trujillo tried to organize them. "Naturally," he said, "Trujillo was the most influential person in the counterrevolution, for he had more money than the others as well as a center of operations with all the needed

Fidel Castro Speaks

facilities." The revolutionary plan of infiltrating the counterrevolutionary elements, Castro said, began to achieve success when William Morgan accepted their proposal. Within three months, Castro declared, William Morgan, Menoyo Carrera, (Fleta.), and all the Escambray commanders were in the plot. The plotters became so confident that they even went to live in William Morgan's house, and "Trujillo appointed William Morgan the leader of the counterrevolutionary." Castro said that William Morgan "displaced Pedraza, Batista, Ventura, (Carrataraz?); in fact he displaced the entire Batista group." Asked whom Trujillo used to make contact with William Morgan and the others Premier Castro said that his contact men included the consul in Miami, "who was one of his principal agents in the conspiracy," and a Spanish priest, Velazco, who lives in Santo Domingo, and in whom "Trujillo has great confidence." This priest, Castro said, went to Havana three times. He "brought 10 bazookas and a large quantity of weapons on one of his trips. Castro declared? "We possess the details of all the incidents because we had 12 of our comrades spend three months living with the counterrevolutionary elements. Their ability was

Fidel Castro Speaks

so great that in three months they committed no indiscretion whatsoever. In short, all men in key positions were our comrades." Castro continued that as the organization of the counterrevolution progressed, "Trujillo sacrificed Nunez Portuondo." He added that "the principal candidate of the 'Rosa Blanca' was Nunez Portuondo." Castro said that the organizers of the plot tried to find a leader for the counterrevolutionary who was in the country and who had had little connection with Batista. Primer Castro declared that "All this is part of a great plot. This is not only the work of Trujillo. Trujillo is just one phase of the giant conspiracy against the revolution." The conspiracy against the Cuban revolution includes vested interests, "of which, unfortunately, many are foreign interests. This makes our struggle more difficult because it is not only the national elements which oppose our aims, but also foreign interests, powerful interests which have an influence in certain political circles in other countries, which influence the press in other for the countries, influence information agencies; interests that have the ability to do great harm, to discredit, picture us in the worse way, slander, confuse, and give the impression that

Fidel Castro Speaks

this is a debacle, and that the most terrible things are done here. "In short, large groups of vested interests are engaged in this maneuver. They have taken an oath to oppose our revolution to the death, to try to isolate us from all other countries, to try and create within and without our country, political and economic, national and international, that is, all kinds of problems for us. This foreign ministers conference is only a part of the conspiracy against our country. In short, these (word indistinct) of events which strangely coincide with the foreign ministers conference again show that all this is only a conspiracy, that all this is only an evil attempt against our country and our revolution." Castro said: "When I asked a Spaniard of the Trujillo legion who had become our prisoner why he came, the first thing he said was that he had been told that we were communists and that he was an enemy of communists." Castro then said that this was the work of those who went abroad to speak against us, such as Diaz Lanz. Declaring that the revolution and the people would never admit defeat, Castro said that in the first place the conspirators should have realized this before making absurd plans against the majority in the

Fidel Castro Speaks

Cuban nation. He added that he was surprised that the enemies of the revolution thought that the revolution would abandon the struggle and permit itself to be overthrown. "They must overthrow us if it is possible to overthrow a united people. They may overthrow us if an entire nation can be liquidated," he said. He then said he wondered how it would be possible to govern the people without an army if they did not have any public support, when Batista had to maintain power by force of arms. He said that thousands of men would go off to the mountains with their weapons to fight against the reestablishment of the Batista regime. Speaking of the corruption during the Batista regime, Castro said that the revolutionary government inherited nothing but debts and that the country had only 70 million pesos in reserve. He declared that in these circumstances the most the government could do is to speed up the agrarian reform, tourist plans, and other plans to give employment to everyone as soon as possible, and to develop an economy that will maintain the Cuban people. A reporter asked Castro what Trujillo's "legion," which Castro had mentioned, was. Castro replied: We have a Spanish member of the legion here. He can tell

Fidel Castro Speaks

you about it; where he contracted for it, who did it, how much he was offered, and what he was told. His contract ended when he was taken prisoner. "He no longer has any agreement with Trujillo, because he is a prisoner." If the reporters want to, we invite you to ask him anything here on television. Castro suggested that the questions be asked later. Castro then stated that the prisoners had been treated according to international law; that they might be tried in court, but never tortured or otherwise mistreated by the revolutionary government. Castro suggested the reporters question William Morgan and Guiterrez Manoyo, and a reporter asked if there was any effort being made to mobilize the pro-Cuban feeling that he was certain existed among non-Cubans, as shown by the activities of William Morgan. Castro replied: "Morgan is a Cuban. He married a Cuban; he is not a North American." Castro then said that there was no organized effort to mobilize this pro-Cuban feeling abroad, but that it had to be done. He noted that movements in support of the Cuban revolution did exist, as could be seen in Latin America while the foreign ministers conference was in progress. "This has not been the product of a methodical effort," he

Fidel Castro Speaks

claimed. Castro then volunteered a statement on the alleged invasion of Haiti by a group of Cuban revolutionaries. He said that several days ago an (Algerian?) man, "an adventurer who was a rebel in Las Villas," enlisted a group of 25 or 30 rebels and left in a boat from the northern part of Oriente Province. "This was something planned by those elements which are conspiring against Cuba," he said. He continued that it seemed that they landed in Haiti. He said that capturing 30 Cubans on an invasion of Haiti, a country whose language and terrain is foreign, must have been a plan to embarrass us at the foreign ministers conference. He went on to say that this has "forced us to make the regretable decision to apply very severe measures against these actions, which are intolerable." Speaking of the conference of foreign ministers, Castro said that "the logical thing" for it to discuss was "the economic problems of Latin America, not interventions or expeditions." He said that "apart from the efforts of our delegation and of the Venezuelan delegation the conference is a farce." He said that Cuba did not want to be defended by an international organization, and that "we cannot and will not hope for foreign aid in defense of

Fidel Castro Speaks

our revolution." Dictators usually hope for and get international aid. He said that Cuba did not need OAS aid, and that the conference had coincided with four invasions of Cuba, "one from the united States and three from Santo Domingo." He said that "two planes had arrived simultaneously at the Trinidad airport, but one did not dare to land." One of the planes came from Santo Domingo and one from Florida, he said, and wondered if, with all the coast guarding resources at the command of the United States, those planes could leave without the "complicity of officials." "I asked myself if it was logical for us to be accused of those things from abroad while during the foreign ministers conference arms shipments were arriving here from the United States and from Santo Domingo? We would really be in a fix if we had to depend on those international organizations for our defense," he said, "because the peoples have never received even minimum aid from those organizations. The foreign ministers never met in a foreign ministers conference for the benefit of peoples, but they meet now as an instrument to maneuver against a country that has liberated itself from tyranny." "What could the goal of that conference be when Trujillo was

Fidel Castro Speaks

represented at the conference? The same Trujillo, who (is trying?) to plot a counterrevolution. "What more proof is necessary than the recordings of broadcasts of La Voz Dominicana at the conference to know whether we can consider as a serious event that conference of foreign ministers which was convoked by Trujillo himself?" "While this conference is going on--a conference called through the intrigue of Trujillo--a counterrevolution is attempted in our country, to disturb the peace, to send plane loads of arms and machineguns, to start a revolution here. All of this simply means that, up to now, unfortunately, they are playing that dictatorship's game, because Trujillo would not worry us one bit--if we knew that we had only to worry about him as a means of provocation. This would also be true if we had to have a fight between the people of Cuba and the Santo Domingo dictatorship. "This," continued Castro, "would not be a problem for us, because we know that the Cubans have enough qualities and have enough energy to liquidate the Trujillo regime in two weeks, if necessary. Trujillo, however, is sheltered by this international organism. He is sheltered in all his international provocative

Fidel Castro Speaks

actions and we remain here with our arms crossed, tolerating the Trujillo planes that (fly?) over our coasts, tolerating the Trujillo planes that threaten to bomb us, and tolerating that Trujillo theft of the planes in which the war criminals fled. We have to allow him to organize attempts against our embassies and be constantly exposed to his provocations." Castro continued: "We have to go on tolerating Trujillo and we have to be exposed to the stupidity and madness of this man, the son of intervention and the protege of international agencies, of the consortium of international interests which keep him in power. "We have our delegation in Chile to explain all these truths. Yet to create more problems for us and to obstruct us, to prevent Cuba from explaining her position at the Santiago conference, counterrevolutions are hatched--counterrevolutions that practically coincide with the foreign ministers conference." Castro blamed Trujillo for inciting some 30 Cubans to provoke, hurt, and demoralize Cuba. "These are the things," he said, "that should open the people's eyes and prove to them that a revolution is not an easy thing, that it is not a little stroll. The people should know that we have to defend ourselves very tenaciously, very

Fidel Castro Speaks

intelligently, and very firmly, since we can count on no one else but ourselves, our own resources, and the sympathy of the people. Nothing more than this, because generally the oligarchies and the vested interests in other countries do nothing else but play the game and abet the enemies of this revolution." Castro then reminded his listeners of life under Batista, when children were tortured and all sorts of crimes were committed. But, he said, news of this kind was never published by the UPI and other international news agencies. Therefore the Cubans are alone in defending themselves. At this point, Castro was asked to explain about a report in a newspaper saying that the counterrevolutionaries had three bases in Florida from which to fight against Cuba. Would it not be possible, a reporter asked, for the government to take steps against this and have the friendly government of the United States help them? "Well," Castro replied, "why waste time? They have taken in the war criminals up there; the bodies of five compatriots were received there; both political and military elements are hiding behind a mask of respectability up there; planes with arms and pamphlets by criminals have left there.

Fidel Castro Speaks

Therefore, it is possible that if the U.S. officials did not want a single plane to take off from there to drop pamphlets here and gather war criminals they could stop them." Castro then said that Maj. William Morgan was offered 40 50-caliber machineguns by Dominican agents. "You can imagine what 40 50-caliber machineguns mean. During the hardest fighting of the Sierra Maestra campaign when we were fighting against all the battalions of the dictatorship last summer we had only two 50-caliber machineguns." In other words, he said, this Dominican gentlemen had had no trouble in acquiring guns and the officials of the state of Florida pretended they knew nothing about it. Yet, when the Cubans were fighting for a just cause, they had to overcome many obstacles--obstacles that the war criminals do not have to contend with. A reporters asked whether Castro would personally attend the Santiago conference in order to denounce the entire Trujillo plot. Castro replied: "The foreign Ministers conference ends Sunday morning and there is no time for me to attend the end of the conference. Because of the things happening here, we thought it our duty to remain here. Moreover, we have a good representative at the conference in the person

Fidel Castro Speaks

of Dr. Raul Roa." The cabinet, he continued, thought that I should remain here as much as possible and try to attend the conference during its later stage. Things took longer than we expected and today is Friday. I could not leave without giving the nation an explanation of the events that have occurred. As I have said, Castro continued, the foreign ministers conference was called through the intrigue of Trujillo. We have proof of it. What shall we propose? Shall we propose that the conference scold Trujillo? Trujillo does not care about any of this. He is supporting the foreign legion; he does not care about public opinion in Santo Domingo; he does not care about public opinion on the continent. We know that the great international interests are not interested in getting Trujillo out of the Dominican Republic but in getting rid of the revolutionary government in Cuba. "You understand," Castro went on "that what the conference is interested in is to destroy the national government. We are not going there to concoct a plan that will work against us. All we can do there, at this international conference, is to ask that Cuba's sovereignty be respected and that the Cuban nation be respected. What else can we hope for?" For example, he continued,

Fidel Castro Speaks

we know of the plan of campaign against Cuba. We know that these powerful agencies with their monopoly on information intervene in the problems of our country place obstacles in the path of tourism, and create many problems for us. They let the conspirators loose against us. At this point a reporter asked Castro about the plot that has just been smashed in Cuba. Castro replied that it had vast ramifications. He said that the plotters abroad counted on the help of military elements in the country and on help from within. "Our plan to foil the invasion," he said, "included four points; namely, to seize the plotters, to seize the money that the landholders and Trujillo had given to the counterrevolution, to seize the arms (received from the United States?), and to destroy the elements that landed here. The plans were realized. All the conspirators were seized. Not a single one of them escaped. The money given by the landholders was also seized. The money was seized for the land reform. Of course, we did not take as much as we had wanted to but we seized some 78,000 dollars." "It was understood," said Castro, "that at the moment of the uprising in Cuba Trujillo would send his legion. All the sectional leaders of the revolt

Fidel Castro Speaks

were given their briefing on Saturday morning; one group was to act in Pinar del Rio and another on Isla de Pinas. The aim of the latter action was to free all the prisoners on the Isla de Pinas. Another group was to take over the Sierra de Escambray and there receive the legion." The chief of the Pinar del Rio and Isla de Pinas, Castro continued, failed to get a seat on the plane and thus failed to mobilize the Isla de Pinas group. He was arrested by Major Menoyo in Morgan's house. All the leaders of the movement were to meet in Morgan's house and receive instructions. Major Menoyo and a group of comrades were living there. When all plans had been made, they were arrested. It so happened, he continued, that one of the plotters in Morgan's house telephoned a Major Carrera in another house, where a group of Cainas Milanes' landholder conspirators was located. Others were to meet with Hernandez Tellaheche and his group. For some reason or other, Hernandez Tellacheche had lost his confidence and had not held this meeting. However, the group that was to meet with Cainas Milanes did meet and they were arrested at the moment he arrived. On the next day all the members of the former armed forces still in service were put

Fidel Castro Speaks

under preventive arrest. Almost all of them have now been freed. "Naturally," Castro added, "we tried to maintain the greatest secrecy about the plot, to make sure that we could smash it. It was impossible, though, to keep the secret forever and the cables began to go out and, with them, all sorts of rumors. I, for example, am a very hardy soul with the UPI. They kill me when I am waging a revolution against someone else and they also kill me when someone else is waging a revolution against me. They always kill me." The foreign news agencies said that Elcuterio Pedraza and Portuondo directed the invading forces. They had the counterrevolutionaries in control of Santiago de Cuba, Castro continued. They also said that Castro has not appeared in public and has not appeared on television for four days. "He is not seen any place, and it is supposed that he has been murdered." The cables made things look black for me. Everything I said was propaganda and I was wrong. "Morgan was in contact with Trujillo in the Dominican Republic, meantime, and he convinced Trujillo that everything was in order. On Wednesday night a plane landed in Trinidad with a certain priest, Velazquez, abroad. Fifteen cases containing bazooka ammunition were

Fidel Castro Speaks

landed, as were nine bazookas, five portable radios, another case with four bazooka shells, 28 cases of 50-caliber shells, 45 cases of 30-caliber shells, and 11 more cases with 50-caliber shells." The landing of the plane was a real picture: Almost all the comrades at the airport were dressed in civilian clothes; those that disembarked from the plane were shouting "Long live Trujillo!" There were embraces. After landing the supplies and the men, the plane flew back to Santo Domingo,which could not contain its joy because the revolution was going well. We were supposed to be completely demoralized because there was no reaction against the Trujillo planes on our part. In the meantime, Trujillo's intelligence chief continued giving instructions by radio. On Thursday we sent Trujillo a false message in the name of Morgan telling him that fighting was taking place at six different points of Cuba. Another false message was sent him saying we need many officers and technicians, as well as soldiers and machineguns. The message added that we needed between 200 and 300 experts experienced in the ways of disorganizing the enemy, which was withdrawing. The message said that reinforcement were needed at once,

Fidel Castro Speaks

however, and that we could not do everything by ourselves. Trujillo replied through his chief of intelligence that everything would be done. Sure enough, another plane arrived with 10 men abroad. They were impressed. The town of Trinidad had been blacked out and a simulated battle was being staged nearby to impress the visitors. The latter explained that the two bombers would come the next day and they asked where we wanted them to bomb. We decided to seize the group. There was resistance, of course, and two men on our side were killed and several wounded. The wounded on both sides were taken to the hospital and given every medical attention. (At this point Castro quotes some of the news reported by La Voz Dominicana on his alleged defeat--Ed.) La Voz Dominicana announced that Fidel Castro had been killed and that Santiago de Cuba and many other Cuban towns were in the hands of the counterrevolutionaries. The station then appealed to "Henry" to continue fighting, for the fate of Cuba was in his hands. He, alone, was responsible for wiping communism from Marti's island. Of course "Henry" was the alleged Dominican agent whom we know as William Morgan, our man. Maj. Gutierrez Menoyo was

Fidel Castro Speaks

also supposed to be a Dominican agent, another lie. A reporter suggested that Dr. Castro had enough information available against Trujillo to produce a "white book" that would convince Trujillo's adherents. Castro replied that on the first day, forty 50-caliber machineguns, twelve-30-caliber machineguns, and many shells were seized from a boat. The second shipment consisted of 100 light 50-caliber machineguns that were parachuted to Cuba. The third shipment consisted of 100 bazookas and parts for bazookas, radios, and so forth. The last shipment consisted of 90 Thompson machineguns, 76 Springfields, seventy-four 50-caliber machineguns and many cases of shells, and other arms. "I tell you," said Castro, "that if we had received all this in the Sierra Maestra I am sure that we would have won the war in a few months." Trujillo is against us, against Venezuela, and against anyone who sees in him a dictator. He respects the citizens of no country. He has not respected the University of Columbia, from which he kidnaped a professor and later murdered him. He has friends; he has the international situation in his favor. If it were up to us to take care of him, he would not last two weeks. He can thank the international

Fidel Castro Speaks

situation prevailing in our continent. Castro then accused Trujillo of dozens of other crimes, saying that he once killed 10,000 Haitians and that the Haitian Government is under his wing. "The best thing that could be done would be to settle accounts with Trujillo. But as things are, we must remain here on the defensive. We must keep waiting for his legion to come, for his planes and arms to come. The international situation keeps our hands tied and we can only wait for Trujillo's provocations." A reporter asked: "Dr. Castro, to call a spade a spade, do you think that the United States is mainly responsible for Trujillo's permanence and the present situation existing in the Caribbean? Do you think that, since the United States is a country where public opinion prevails,and with the proof that the Cuban Government has, that U.S. opinion will be mobilized and bring about a change in the stupid policy pursued by the State Department in Trujillo's case?" U.S. public opinion must bring about a change in policy with respect to Trujillo, Castro answered. Public opinion in the United States is against Trujillo. The U.S. State Department has to resolve the problem. Part of the difficulty stems from the fact that the OAS had been ineffective in its efforts to

Fidel Castro Speaks

preserve human rights. "The worst of the OAS is that it can be converted into an instrument against a revolutionary government such as ours." Our republics are a group of poor nations. They should all extend a hand to one another to resolve the very grave economic crises. We should cooperate and not be victims of competition. Only in this way can the nations of Latin America develop. Cuba is being blamed for existing problems, but the one who should have been blamed for the past 30 years is Trujillo, gentlemen. "We see the possibility that the OAS can be converted into an instrument against the Cuban revolution and we cannot promote or accept in any way a policy which aims at resolving through intervention the problem of Cuba and that of Santo Domingo." Santo Domingo could be used to involve Cuba also in a conflagration. Cuba is not to be blamed; Cuba is a victim. Trujillo is a gangster and the OAS can do nothing. The OAS is paying the consequences of its neglect of peoples, of its forgetfulness of human rights. All of America is paying for the consequences of its errors. We have no other ally but that of public opinion on the continent. The natural ally of our revolution is public opinion. We have no other alternative

Fidel Castro Speaks

but to let everyone know that we are ready to defend the revolution and to defend the nation with all the necessary means." (There was a pause as prisoners were brought in for questioning.) The prisoners were asked how they came to join the counterrevolution and if they realized Trujillo was an international criminal. One prisoner was asked if he could see any signs of communism since he came to Cuba or did he now believe he had been deceived. He replied that he saw no indication of communism in Cuba. Questioned on the composition of the Trujillo foreign legion to which he was affiliated, a prisoner replied that it consisted mostly of Spaniards but that other Europeans were also included. The next prisoner questioned, a Cuban, said his name was Pedro Rivero Moreno. He was asked if he was willing to reply to questions and replies in the affirmative. He said that some Cubans and Spaniards were involved in the plot. He was a former army officer. He was in the foreign legion in the Dominican Republic and never thought of coming to Cuba. There are perhaps two or three Cubans in the Dominican army, he said. It was not his decision to come to Cuba, but he was told to take some weapons to Commander

Fidel Castro Speaks

William Morgan and that he was to go as a technician; he made several trips of this nature. Information concerning the foreign legion followed. Rivero Moreno said that it was a separate unit having its own uniform and was not commanded by Dominican army officers. He said that he was chief of the security service but that no one knows Trujillo's plans. They are secret. Another Cuban prisoner questioned said that he was willingly giving information. He said that he had had some political experience, and that he felt that he could have a political future in Cuba again since he had never done anything bad. He said there were 25,000 men in the foreign legion. Asked about how much has been spent in propaganda and in weapons to be used against the present Cuban Government, he said that very few had contributed to it. He said that Masferrer was plotting against Cuba. Castro then summed up that the rebel army had done well. Imagine, it has been working on this for three months and did not make a single mistake. Its action was quite intelligent, and it maintained the same moral principles of the war. The prisoners were treated well. When it was necessary to act, every one of the conspirators was captured. There was no

Fidel Castro Speaks

violence, and this shows that to defend the revolution it is possible to use what one may call rebel proceedings. These are absolutely clean and legal and lead to the discovery of everything. Most of the prisoners have been seized. It would be impossible to try them all. Only the leaders will be tried. The others will be deferred as soon as possible to the ordinary courts. Castro concluded that the revolution is so strong that the country can remain calm in the face of any threat or plot. We shall use the means at our disposal to repel any attack. Cruelty, violence, and humiliations are not necessary. Only correct investigating methods are needed and these have given the best results.

Fidel Castro Speech at Loyalty Rally
Workers, farmers, students, all Cubans: We have a lot to talk over with you. In this great rally today there are important matters to be dealt with. This is or should be more than just a moment of enthusiasm. It should be above all a time of meditation. Every nation must search for the source of its problems. It is not enough to know the facts. It is necessary for the people to know the factors behind the facts. The support

Fidel Castro Speaks

of the people gratifies us. There extraordinary enthusiasm gives us satisfaction. But, above all it interests us that the people should meditate. It interests us that the people should think because the people should find an explanation for the problems with which they are confronted. I am not here to make a speech. I am here to reason with the people. I am here to converse with the people. Never has there been a time when it was more necessary that there should be the most complete understanding between the people and us. After all, those of us who make up the Council of Ministers and occupy the key positions of the government are merely men of the people. We are simply carrying out the will of the people and fulfilling the desires of the people. Never has there been a time when it was more necessary that the Cuban people and we, the revolutionary leaders, should think and act as one. If our enemies engage us in battle we will give them battle. If they attack us they will find all of Cuba to be one great army. We are not dismayed by deserters and cowards. After all we have just been through a war. In the war we learned that some men desert and some men turn cowards; but they do not matter because they are the minority. We know that we

Fidel Castro Speaks

have with us the people of Cuba and the people are not going to become cowardly. There is only one way for our people to obtain victory and make progress--through courage. We know that the people will not become cowardly. We know that the people are willing to die alongside their revolutionary government. The people know that we can end this struggle only by winning or by dying in the attempt. The people know perfectly well that the men who today have the reins of the government in their hands, these rebels who have appeared today on this platform, are men who are willing to die alongside the people. When the people of a nation are courageous and willing to face death, when their leaders are willing to die with them, that nation is invincible; that nation cannot be overcome by anything or anybody. These are the questions we should ask ourselves: Why are we being attached? Why have we had to meet here together again? Why are there traitors? Why is there an attempt to make the revolution fail? What accusations are being made against the Revolution? Why are certain charges made against us? What ends are being sought? How should the people contend with these maneuvers and motives? How can the success of the Revolution be

Fidel Castro Speaks

assured? What measures have we taken and what measures are we willing to take in order to defend the Revolution? Before going further I want to defend the Revolution? "UPI 3:38 p.m. Officials of the customs of Miami are investigating the news that six or seven airplanes are in flight from the Miami area toward Havana to drop counterrevolutionary leaflets over the rally in support of Castro being carried out in Havana. Customs official Joseph Portier said that he had information that these flight were being made but he did not know what success they may have had. "'We are trying to place agents in these possible flights,' Portier said. He also said that he had sent agents to various airports of the meridional region of Florida and that some of the airplanes that took part in the alleged flight to Havana were rented and others were private property." I read this bulletin for the simple reason that I know that the people are not afraid. But at the same time while we have been here on this platform we have received the following communication from the head of the regiment of the Rebel Army in the Province of Pinar del Rio: "Be advised that an avionette has flown over the city and (from it) were thrown hand made grenades as well as an

Fidel Castro Speaks

incendiary bomb at the Niagara Sugar Mill. A
house was set on fire between the post office
and the Army garrison. It was at six thirty in the
evening. They also dropped pamphlets." That is
to say, the very authorities of Miami recognized
that six or seven airplanes left from that area en
route to Cuba and that they were still waiting for
the results of the flights. Very well. Now we can
give the first report of the results. And we beg
them, if they will be so kind, to go ahead and
send along the official war communique letting
us know the pilots' tally of this daring sortie
against the people of Cuba. This is the limit. We
cannot be sure whether it is shamelessness or
whether is it complete impotence on the part of
the United States that the authorities should
report news of the fifth aerial bombing mission
over our territory. How is it possible that the
authorities of a nation so powerful, with so many
economic and military resources, with radar
systems which are said to be able to intercept
even guided missiles, should admit before the
world that they are unable to prevent aircraft
from leaving their territory in order to bomb a
defenseless country like Cuba? I wonder--and
this is a question we should all ask ourselves in
order to find an explanation for what is

Fidel Castro Speaks

happening... I wonder if the authorities of the United States would be so negligent as to permit Russian emigrants from Alaska to carry out bombing raids over cities and villages of Russian territory. I ask myself if they would be so careless as to permit that act of aggression from their territory. Next I ask myself how it is possible then that the authorities of the United States should be so careless that on the other hand they do permit these aerial attacks against a country of their own Continent--permit this aggression against a small and weak country that has no resources to defend itself from those attacks, and has no military power. I ask myself if the cause for this neglect is that we are a weak nation. Are the authorities of the powerful nations careful not to permit acts of aggression against other powerful nations, and yet do they on the other hand permit these acts against nations like us? I can see no other explanation. I cannot conceive of any explanation other than the fact that Cuba is a small nation unable to defend itself from those attacks, a country that is not a world power. I am unable to find--and I do not believe that there is--any other explanation, because the honorable attitude for powerful nations would be to make certain to prevent

Fidel Castro Speaks

their territory from serving as a base for aggression against a smaller country... as well as to prevent raids against a powerful country. Who are those who attack us from the United States and why do they attack us? When I contemplate these problems I cannot avoid remembering the first days after we won the war. I cannot avoid remembering the overwhelming joy of our people, the infinite happiness of the Cuban people. I remember they were happy because the war was over and because no more blood was going to be spilled, because no more homes and no more villages wee going to be burned, because the murderous bombings were not going to be repeated again. Our people were happy because they had obtained peace. Our people were happy because none of them could ever suspect that some day from foreign territory, the criminals, the same merciless hordes who cowardly fled the first of January, would return with their inconceivably inhuman methods to spread terror among our people. It is painful to remember those days because they remind us of a happy people who believed that never again would they have to suffer terror at the hands of that group of criminals that we had

Fidel Castro Speaks

finally driven out of power. But why do they attack us? And what is the reason for the tolerance of the American authorities? On another occasion like this when all the people were assembled here to defend our country from an organized campaign of libel and slander, I said that our enemies were using defamation in the press in order to lay the way for acts of aggression against us. The months have not yet passed by and we have had to call the people together again. This time not just to defend ourselves from slander, but to struggle for the very survival of our citizens, and in defense of the safety of our children. What we can depend upon we have mobilized. We have mobilized the Cuban people. We have gathered a million Cubans together on three days' notice, to proclaim before all the nations of the world, our protest against the acts of barbarity which, in one afternoon and in the course of just a few minutes, produced 47 victims among our unwarned and defenseless civilians. But why are we attacked? Why don't airplanes fly out of Florida to attack the dictatorship of Trujillo? Why don't airplanes leave the United States to attack the dictatorship of Somoza? Of course, airplanes should not leave the United States to

Fidel Castro Speaks

bomb us here nor bomb anybody, anywhere! They should not go to Santo Domingo nor to Nicaragua. They should not go anywhere. But what we must ask ourselves is: Why precisely is Cuba chosen? After all, there are emigrants of all nationalities in the United States--even many emigrants from our sister nation Puerto Rico, that has the right to aspire to be one more independent nation in Latin America. And, nevertheless, although there are many emigrants from many nations, Cuba just happens to be the one country to which airplanes depart with emigrants abroad to attack a civil population. Why precisely Cuba? If there is one country with which the United States should be more careful, if there is one country about which the United States should be concerned that these incidents should not occur, this country is Cuba. Cuba has just been through a two years was during which airplanes of American origin were used to drop on Cuban cities and on the Cuban countryside rocket projectiles and incendiary bombs also of American manufacture. Thousands of our people were murdered with weapons of American manufacture. The least we could expect after having destroyed Batista's

Fidel Castro Speaks

mercenary army, after we liberated our people from tyranny, the least that we could expect is that our people should not continue to be bombed from bases located in the territory of the United States. What can we think of such negligence on the part of the authorities of a country which right here, in the heart of our country, maintains a naval base to protect its citizens from an attack of any kind? How is it possible that the return (for the use of Guantanamo as a naval base the American Government does not prevent) bases located in the United States (from being used to subject us) to attacks carried out by our war criminals who are harbored in the United States? How is it possible that in return for the risks we run with the presence of that military base in our country, the cottages of our farmers, our sugar mills, and our civil population are exposed to incendiary bombs and to machine-gunning from airplanes that come here from the United States? What would be the reaction of the American public if the American public were aware of all this? In the name of the people of Cuba I appeal to the public opinion of the United States. I do not conceive nor believe that the people of the United States could approve of

Fidel Castro Speaks

such irresponsibility on the part of the authorities of their country. I ask myself what would happen, what would the people of the United States say if planes departing from Canada or any other country should drop incendiary bombs on American factories and houses and then make a raid on the capital of the United States, with the result that city hospitals would be crowded with men, children and old people, wounded by machineguns. The people of the United States still have fresh in their memory the treacherous surprise attack on Pearl Harbor. I am sure that under no circumstances would the American people, who experienced such profound indignation over Pearl Harbor, approve these aerial attacks (on Cuba) nor would they by any means accept the explanation that the authorities are unable to prevent these flights. As I said a few days ago, the people of the United States would have to come to the conclusion that either their authorities are accomplices to the raids on Cuba or the American nation has been deceived by its authorities, and is defenseless. How is it possible that the American people can be told that they are safe even from guided missiles if the government is not even capable of

Fidel Castro Speaks

preventing small aircraft from taking off and landing as they please from their territory? Guantanamo Naval Base. Another question that we must ask ourselves is: What do our enemies expect to accomplish with these bombings? Do they simply want to make us live in a constant state of fear never knowing at what hour of the day they can scatter death and destruction among us? This in itself would be sadism and vengeance (characteristic of our war criminals). But what we all suspect is even worse: that by using surprise bombings they think they can finally bring about such a state of fear and cowardice among our people that we might abandon our Revolution and--by turning the government over to mercenaries and reactionaries--deliver Cuba back into the hands of the Masferrers, the Pilar Garcias, the Venturas, the Carratalas. On one hand, Cuba is being threatened by economic strangulation, that is to say, the loss of the sugar quota which provides our principal income. On the other hand, we are being subjected to aerial attacks that have the objective of terrorizing us so that we will renounce our magnificent revolutionary reform program and give up our hope of creating social justice here in our island. What

Fidel Castro Speaks

has the Revolutionary Government of Cuba
done to deserve this aggression against us?
Our internal problems and our international
problems simply result from opposition to the
Revolution itself. It is our process of
revolutionary reform that has caused
aggressions from outside Cuba as well as
treason inside Cuba. What has the
Revolutionary Government done? The only
accusation that can be made against the
revolutionary Government is that we have given
our people reform laws. Everything we have
done can be reviewed with pride by our people.
Why are the people of Cuba with us? Not just
for purely sentimental reasons. The people
support the Revolutionary Government because
we have passed revolutionary reform laws. Why
do the farmers support the Revolutionary
Government? Why do the workers support the
Revolutionary Government? Why do the
immense majority of the people support the
Revolutionary Government? Who do the people
defend the Revolutionary Government? Simply
because we have been defending the people,
because we have been carrying out reforms in
Cuba. Here in public we are going to give our
answer once and for all to those who slander

and belittle the revolution. They will finally have to remove their masks; they will have to admit that the accusations they make --that we are communists-- can be attributed exclusively to the fact that they have not dared to admit that they are against our reform program. Since there are no just complaints or accusations that can be made against our government, our enemies resort to that old bugaboo that they have been using for the last 50 years. They label us falsely as best suits their schemes to commit aggression against us, and thus they proceed, aided and abetted by foreign interests that are our enemies. What we must analyze is what the Revolutionary Government has done and what we must ask is whether the people of Cuba are in agreement with that the Revolutionary Government has been doing. Do you approve of our having given you honest administration of public funds for the first time in the history of Cuba? Do you approve of our having put an end to smuggling? Do you approve of our having abolished the practice of payroll padding in the offices of the government? Do you approve of our having eradicated gambling from the daily life of our average citizen? Do you approve of our having

Fidel Castro Speaks

tried and executed guilty war criminals by firing squads? Do you approve of our having recovered property that was embezzled during the dictatorship? Do you approve of our having converted the headquarters of the old Political Police into a children's playground and of our having changed the old Army headquarters into a scholastic center that the children of Cuba so needed? Do you approve of our having converted army regimental headquarters into other schools? Do you approve of our having cancelled the dishonest concession that the dictatorship gave to the Telephone Company? Do you approve of our having put the price of medicine within the reach of the people? Do you approve of our having created ten thousands more jobs for teachers out in the rural areas? Do you approve of our having founded the National Institute of Savings and Housing which has already built 10,000 homes? Do you approve of our having provided a Social Security Bank? Do you approve of our having taken steps to develop the tourist industry on a large scale as an important source of income for our country? Do you approve of our having returned to the workers their union rights and all the other benefits that were taken away from

Fidel Castro Speaks

them during the tyranny? Do you approve of our having reduced the rents so that every family could have a place of their own? Do you agree that it was right for us to give boats to the fishermen so they could keep the profits from their own work and stop being exploited? Do you approve of the consumers' cooperatives that we have organized in the country to prevent the farmers from being charged the double prices they have always been charged? Are you in favor of the Land Reform? Do you approved of our having given land to the farmers? Do you agree that it is right that the farmers who produce charcoal, in Cienaga de Zapata, Peninsula de Guanachahabibes, Belice, Yateras and many other parts of Cuba should have cooperatives where they can sell their charcoal, rather than being exploited as they always have been? Do you approve of our having built decent housing for the farmers and of our having constructed highways and schools from one end of the island to the other? Were you in favor of the old system of rural police at the service of the big landlords and the monopolies? Or are you in favor of the soldiers of the Revolutionary Army who are today the allies and friends of the farmers? The Rebel

Fidel Castro Speaks

Army does not commit injustices. The Rebel Army works exclusively in behalf of the people. Do you approve of our having helped the farmers go back to the rural areas that had become abandoned as a result of the greed and selfishness of the big landlords? Do you agree that it was right for us to protect our monetary reserves in order to make funds available to industrialize the country? Do you agree that we are right in insisting that the country import tractors now instead of Cadillacs? Do you agree with us that it is right for us to plant as much rice as we can instead of importing it? and produce as much lard as we can instead of importing it? and produce all the cotton we can instead of importing it? all the foodstuffs we can instead of importing them? and in this way provide jobs for more than half a million of our fellow Cubans who are unemployed? Do you approve of our plans to industrialize the country? Then, I ask: has the Revolutionary Government done anything that the people do not approve? What has the Revolutionary Government done except defend the interests of the people? What have we done except sacrifice ourselves for our country? In four centuries of Cuban history never has there been such an altruistic movement. In the 1500's the Indians of this island were persecuted and slaughtered by the Spanish conquistadores. For over three hundred years during the colonial period there was slavery in Cuba and human beings were bought and sold like animals. Our own seven year struggle against tyranny cost 20,000 lives, while thousands of homes were destroyed by fire thanks to selfishness, greed and vested interests. At long last the destiny of Cuba is being shaped by a revolutionary movement which is fighting against inequality and injustice--a revolutionary government which is determined to redeem our people and to destroy evils which, in some instances, have been in existence for more than four hundred years. The Revolutionary Government of Cuba has begun to build what has not been built during the 50 years that this country has been a republic--streets, water works, schools, hospitals, and industries. What have the people of Cuba and its Revolutionary Government done except defend Cuban interests in Cuba and abroad? I ask myself and ask you if the worthy and courageous position taken by the people of Cuba in the international organizations is or is not correct? I could go on asking whether or not you approve of our having given the common people the right to use those beaches which used to belong only to a small privileged group, so that now with all stupid prejudices abolished all Cubans can go to the beaches, whatever color their skin may be. I ask you whether or not you approve of our having given all Cubans, whatever color their skin may be, an equal opportunity to work. We could go on indefinitely asking what has the Revolutionary Government done that is not for the benefit of the people. The problem is: if we plant rice, we interfere with foreign interests; if we produce lard, we interfere with foreign interests; if we produce cotton, we interfere with foreign interests, if we cut down the electric tariffs, we interfere with foreign interests; if we make a Petroleum Law, like the one which is about to be decreed, we interfere with foreign interests; if we carry out a Land Reform, we interfere with foreign interests; if we make a Mining Law, like the one which is about to be announced, we interfere with foreign interests; if we create a Merchant Marine, we interfere with foreign interests. If we try to find new markets for our country, we interfere with foreign interests. If we attempt to sell at least as much as we buy, we interfere with foreign

Fidel Castro Speaks

interests. Because our Revolutionary Laws have an adverse effect on privileged classes inside Cuba and outside Cuba, they attack us and attack us and call us Communists. They accuse us, trying to find some pretext to justify aggression against our country. By any change is the Land Reform Law not (good for) Cubans? By any change is the reduction of excessive electricity rates not (good for) Cubans? By any change is the reduction of excessive telephone rates not (good for) Cubans? Is it by any change not (good for) Cuba that we make an effort to create a Merchant Marine? Is it by any change not (good for) Cuba to plant rice and cotton and to produce lard in our country? Is it by any change not (good for) Cuba to build houses for our workers, our farmers, and the Cuban families in general? Is it by any change not (good for) Cuba to reduce the price of medicines, many of which come from foreign laboratories? Is it or is it not (good for) Cuba to defend our monetary reserves? Is it or is it not (good for) Cuba to buy tractors instead of Cadillacs? Is it or is it not (good for) Cuba to provide ten thousand schools--which is twice the number that had been provided in the fifty years that Cuba has been a Republic? Is it or is it not

Fidel Castro Speaks

(good for) Cuba to convert our fortresses into scholastic centers? Is it or is it not (good for) Cuba to give boats to our fishermen? To give equipment to our farmers? To give our workers what is due them? Is it or is it not (good for) Cuba to proclaim it the duty of Cubans to consume Cuban products? Is it or is it not (good for) Cuba to protect our national industries? Are the measures adopted by the Revolutionary Government not Cuban, or are they the very essence of Cubanism? Then, what do those wretched conspirators charge us with? Of what can those criminals, those false and shameless men (like Diaz Lanz and Huber Matos) accuse us, except of having undertaken measures for the benefit of Cuba? What do not (serve the interest of) Cuba are the foreign monopolies. What does not (serve the interests of) Cuba is the Electric Company. What does not (serve the interests of) Cuba is the Telephone Company. Nor does the United Fruit Company. Nor does the Atlantic and Gulf Company. Nor do the contracts to foreign shipping companies that carry cargo into and out of our ports. The greater part of the rice we consume, the greater part of the lard we consume, the greater part of the textile products

Fidel Castro Speaks

we use, the greater part of the manufactured items we use give profit to others not to Cuba. Those trusts which operate our mines and which have obtained unfair concessions here (give profits to others), not to Cuba. Those companies which were handed over the concessions to exploit most of our land with possible oil wealth (would give profit to others) not to Cuba. The bombs which killed our farmers during the war were (manufactured elsewhere), not in Cuba. The arms and ammunition with which 20,000 of our countrymen were killed were (manufactured elsewhere), not in Cuba, and were not (good for) Cuba. The men who trained the mercenary army destroyed by our Revolution, were not Cuban and were not (good for) Cuba. The campaign of lies and slander being carried out against us does not (originate in) Cuba and is not (good for) Cuba. Those magazines which seek to degrade our people, those international news agencies which write about non-existent horrors in our country, are not Cuban and are not (good for) Cuba. This is the truth, this is the truth which must be told to the people. This is the truth which the false and shameless refuse to admit. They refuse to admit that they are spreading their poison in a campaign against

Fidel Castro Speaks

our Revolution simply because we have taken measures for the good of Cuba. All the great vested interests, both national and international all the enemies of our country have banded together under the same pirates' flag and screaming the same battlecry. Do the reactionaries by any chance want us to give military training to the farmers and the workers? No, certainly not. You have probably noticed the attitude of the mouthpieces of the reactionaries such as this new mouthpiece which pretends to represent the Autentico Abstencionista party, which indeed it does not represent, because the real representative of the Partido Autentico Abstencionista is Dr. Carlos Prio Socarras and he is here with us. Those who publish this new newspaper have allowed themselves to be seduced by the siren song of Diario de la Marina and Avance. And what has this new newspaper done? One of the first things is to join forces with the traitor Huber Matos. In the second place, it tries to make the same insinuations accusing the Revolutionary Government of being Communist. In the third place it prints: "The Revolution, in order to defend itself from its enemies, does not need to arm the workers and the farmers, especially when the proven

Fidel Castro Speaks

courage and skill of the Rebel Army is taken into account and inasmuch as the Revolutionary Government has the moral support of all the people and of all the country." And a few lines further along they print: "If the above is not taken into consideration in a democracy, it would be necessary to continue using the tactic of calling rallies of the masses--a tactic so risky and so tedious for the country when peace and order are more important". Peace in the face of criminal bombing and machine-gunning of our people! It is good to be aware of their attitude in order that the real Autenticos, those who used to constitute the strength of the Autentico Party, may never allow themselves to fall under the influence of those gullible individuals who have been misled by the schemes of La Marina and Avance, gullible individuals who have allowed themselves to be pushed along by the mouthpieces of the reactionaries and the counterrevolutionaries and who are now parroting the same arguments as Trujillo, the Rosa Blanca and the international monopolies that are working against Cuba. As I said before, the people should not allow themselves to be confused. It is money of the robber barons that has brought out this new sheet. I said that we

Fidel Castro Speaks

should carefully contemplate the whys and wherefores of the attacks against us. Why is there such opposition to our training the workers and the farmers? It is very simple. The reactionaries would like for us to have an army such as they supported in what they would call the "good old days". They would like a professional army, such as Cuba used to have. That would be their only hope because such an army down through the years might come to be an instrument of the reactionaries. They have hopes of being able to find somebody greedy for power, some traitor like the one we have just discovered. They have the hope that in a career army they might some day be able to corrupt soldiers and officers, and they have the hope that in the moment least suspected the armed forces of the Republic might determine the fate of our country, because they remember that the big trusts, the vested interests, the robber barons and other power groups and cliques affected by the revolution, all those selfish minorities, are accustomed to using the army as their tool. The army was the instrument of the foreign interests and of the worst elements in our own country. It was no accident that the army of Cuba had foreign instructors. Since they know that a tremendous revolutionary force resides in the people, since they know that civilians with military training could defend all they have won for themselves, the old privileged classes are allergic to everything that is implied by the military training of workers and farmers. On the other hand, we believe that the best allies of the soldiers are the farmers and the workers. In our opinion the best ally of the army is the average citizen. The best troops of the rebel army are the farmers. The officers' clique that supported the traitor Huber Matos were not the kind of soldiers and officers of rural origin who are the pride of the Rebel Army. Huber Matos' accomplices did not belong to the most invincible, to the most courageous, nor to the most steadfast of the Rebel Army. Huber Matos. The fine soldiers who have gone with their rifles and machine guns up to rooftops to improvise anti-aircraft defense of their fellow citizens are soldiers from the Sierra Maestra. They are the "guajiros" from the Sierra Maestra who used to make up the front lines. Those soldiers are true rebels. Why? Because they themselves used to live in the country. They were born in the country and they grew up in the country. They have seen the rural police wield

Fidel Castro Speaks

the butts of their rifles and the backs of their machetes in the interest of the mighty landlords. In the rural parts of Cuba these rebel soldiers have been the hopeless poverty of our farmers. They have seen the horrible spectacle of barefoot, diseased children. In the countrysides of Cuba these guajiro soldiers were acquainted with all the innate goodness and all the heroism of the underprivileged farmers. Nobody will be able to use these rebel soldiers either against the rural population, nor against the civil population in general, because these soldiers do truly understand the spirit of the revolution. It has been their lot to live through and suffer under the conditions that made this revolution necessary. They gave an example to all the farmers of the country and they led the nation to victory. Workers and others citizens of Havana, the riffles that protect you are the rifles of the guajiro soldiers from the Sierra Maestra. And workers, students, farmers, and all the rest of you Cubans with patriotism and love for your country, if the time should come to give battle to defend our rights as Cubans, and to defend the sovereignty of the Cuban nation, you may be sure that those soldiers who are here in Havana protecting you and all the rest of our Rebel Army

Fidel Castro Speaks

would want to have you shoulder to shoulder alongside them. The reactionaries do not want this. What the reactionaries would like is an unarmed civil population and an army which is corruptible and that some day may be able to put a brake on the revolution and make our country backslide. This is why the betrayal of Huber Matos is such a serious matter. It was the first attempt to utilize members of the Rebel Army against the revolution; it was the first attempt to corrupt officers, to use them against the people, against the interests of the people, against the Cuban revolution. Of course the reactinaries do not want the workers and farmers to be given military training. Because they always have the hope that if the country's only defense is a professional army, they might some day be able to win over some officers. They might be able some day to corrupt a professional army and once again have an instrument with which to perpetrate another coup d'etat, like the 10th of March. But there will never again be a 10th of March in our country. The concept of the professional army as the only defense of a country is diametrically opposed to our revolutionary concept that the nation should be safeguarded by the people,

Fidel Castro Speaks

with all the strength of the people and all their love for their country. What do the traitors do? What is the first thing that they do? Repeat the same battlecry as Trujillo, repeat the same battlecry as the Rosa Blanca. Repeat the same battlecry as the criminals of war. Repeat the same battlecry as the international monopolies that are enemies of Cuba. They are accuse the Revolutionary Government of being Communist. What the traitors do first of all is to say "Trujillo, you were right!" That is to say to the war criminals, "you were right". That is to say to the big foreign trusts, "you were right". That is to say to the Rosa Blanca, "you were right". That is to say to those who are bombing our territory, "you were right". The first that they do is to hoist up the same pirates' flag as the war criminals, as the Trujillistas, and the Rosa Blanca. And still they object when we call them traitors! What ends do they pursue with all this? The purpose of dividing the people, of confusing the people, of weakening the nation. Traitors that they are, they want to confuse the people when it is most important for the people to think clearly, and to be aware of what are Cuba's best interests, and of what are the interests of our enemies, of those who cannot share the feelings of our people. Traitors that they are, they take up the standard of the Trujillos, of the war criminals and of the international vested interests who are enemies of Cuba. All those that join forces with the traitors are traitors. And all those who at this moment have the gall to preach disunity of the people, are traitors! All they would accomplish if they could weaken the nation would be to make the powerful enemies of our Revolution feel encouraged to attack us. I say that those who are to be blamed for the bombs are not only those who drop them, but those who right here (in Cuba) inspire the attacks, those who--like Pepin Rivero, of the Diario de la Marina and especially those at Avance--, have been encouraging the counterrevolutionaries. Treason is committed by all those who join forces with the traitors. Why do they do it? Because they oppose our revolutionary reforms. It is not me whom they oppose. It is not the president of the Republic whom they oppose. It is not Raul, Che, Camilo, Almeida, Efigenio Ameijeiras whom they oppose. We are the targets but it is the revolutionary reform program that they oppose. If we had not passed revolutionary laws, they would dedicate the greatest praise to us. Their attack is against the

Fidel Castro Speaks

revolution and the revolutionary laws. It is because of the reform program that they accuse us. I have shown that the laws that are being carried out are truly Cuban and are of benefit to Cubans. What are not Cuban are the selfish interests which oppose the revolutionary laws. Moreover, who are carrying forward this revolution? Who are the men together with me on this platform? While I listened to the words of our revolutionary leaders on this platform, when I heard Major Camilo Cienfeugos, Major Guevara, Major Raul Castro, and Major Almeida, and when I heard our other fellow veterans of the rebel army like Universo Sanchez, Efigenio Ameijeiras and others, I remembered the early fighting phase of the revolution in the Sierra Maestra. I remembered those days of tremendous difficulty, of untold hardships, when such a small group remained steadfast. I was reminded of those days of hunger and cold when we had no coats to shield us from the rain, and no blankets in which to wrap ourselves, to escape from the dampness and the cold of the mountains, those days when we hardly had shoes on our feet and only a few bullets for our rifles, while we were pursued by droves of soldiers. I remember those first days

Fidel Castro Speaks

when the Revolution was thwarted and we were overcome because we were so few. I remember those days in which, with the absolute faith of men who have dedicated themselves to a great and good cause, we persevered, we continued our struggle without becoming demoralized although we were so few in number; here on this platform I have been reminded of those days because I saw here those men who were pillars of strength in the truly difficult, the truly bitter hours. I looked back on all that epic that those faithful revolutionaries wrote. I looked back on it from the first days of Moncada to the invasion, in which two columns under the command of two of the majors who have just spoken to you here, crossed the plans of Camaguey to take help to the fellow rebels who were fighting there, and wrote one of the most glorious pages of military history. That feat would have to be compared with the great feats of the great generals of history. And they are not generals; they are only majors. We have abolished the rank of generals and colonels that used to be a curse to Cuba. Twelve who survived the "Gramma" landing, Dec., 1956. When I listened to our faithful revolutionaries here, I said to myself: "Where are the twelve?"

Fidel Castro Speaks

Of the twelve, several fell in battle, the others are here. The Revolution has had no deserters among the real revolutionaries. Huber Matos, who betrayed us at the approach of the climax of the ASTA Convention, in the midst of the extraordinary effort that we had put forth, is one of the latecomers. Huber Matos is one of those who came into the war, not for the sake of this country, but for his own ulterior motives. He is one of those who went to war not to make his country great but to gain notice for himself. We cannot say that a revolutionary deserted, when he deserted. The day that would be sad would be the day that some of those who were the heart of the Revolution should fail us--the day that one of those who came with us in the "Gramma" should fail us, or the day that there would be a deserter among those who shared all our reverses with us and who have come this far without hesitation. Furthermore, when I see the other officers of the Rebel Army, the other leaders of the revolutionary organizations, for example, the leaders of the University Students League, I feel assured that the revolution is stronger than ever and more united than ever. On what side do we always find the good soldiers? Where will the good revolutionaries

Fidel Castro Speaks

always be? On the side of the people. When I see a million ardent fellow citizens here, I realize that the revolution is stronger than ever, and that the stab in the back just received, far from weakening the revolution, has strengthened it. These traitors assume importance only because they have behind them all the resources of the reactionaries, all the reactionary press here in Cuba and all the press of the international oligarchy. All the resources of the counterrevolution are behind them. They are no more than peons of the counterrevolution, miserable instruments whose statements are given space only in the newspapers that are mouthpieces of the counterrevolution, mouthpieces of the reactionaries. This is not a struggle between individuals. It is a struggle of vested interests, of big trusts against the interests of the Cuban people. That is why the reactionaries do not praise Cuba. Naturally, the reactionaries do not praise Camilo. The reactionaries do praise the traitors. The reactionaries do not praise Almeida. The reactionaries do not praise loyal men. The reactionaries praise the traitors. The reactionaries do not praise the men of ideals. With loyal men, with men of ideals, they can accomplish nothing. The reactionaries glorify the great traitors. The reactionaries do not praise steadfast men. They praise men who surrender, men who give up, men who become cowardly, men who sell out. Some men sell out for money, others for adulation; still others for both money and adulation. But in what company do we find those who so perversely, so shamelessly, accuse the government of being Communist? What do they do but repeat the same battlecry as the Trujillos, the Rosa Blanca, and the other enemies of our country? Do they think that they are going to intimidate us, or do they fail to understand how convinced we are of the justice of the measures that we are taking? Do they fail to understand that we are so firmly convinced that we are serving our people, that only be depriving us of life itself --and not even then-- will they ever be able to suppress our ideals? The reactionaries--those who bomb Cuba, those who drop bombs with the same pretext that the traitors repeat today--are lusting after sensation. What they want is a sensational counterrevolutionary show. What they want are traitors to make the worst charges against the Government so that these charges may be printed in the headlines of their newspaper in

Fidel Castro Speaks

order to spread confusion, in order to weaken the Revolution. No, they don't write a word against the bombs, or if they do they use on what they write the lukewarm touch (characteristic) of those who file reports to satisfy appearances and to disguise their position. The position of those who bomb us in Havana cannot be disassociated from the position of those who betrayed us in Camaguey. When the former deserted, they first wrote a letter for publication in the newspaper; when the latter deserted they also wrote a letter for publication and used the same arguments that were used by traitor Diaz Lanz. The counterrevolutionary press printed Diaz Lanz's statements accusing us as Communists and printed all of Huber Matos's statements accusing us as Communists. The end result of that plot was the dropping of bombs and would have been the releasing of rivers of blood on Cuban soil. This betrayal and the libel by Huber Matos is as ignominious as that of Diaz Lanz, and the worst is the moment that he chose. He did the same in the Sierra Maestra; when the troops were already on the march and he knew that our interest in the offensive would make me restrain myself, he sent his insolent letter to me.

Fidel Castro Speaks

And now, in the middle of the ASTA Convention, when he knew the extraordinary interest of all Cuba in making a success of the visit of those tourist agents, he thought that we would restrain ourselves this time too; so he took the first steps with his plot. But those plans were wrecked with the help of the people, (of Camaguey) not the rabble as the reactionaires call the people. When we began to govern Cuba, there were only seventy million dollars in monetary reserves in the banks. Now that we are making an extraordinary effort, when even the school children contribute their pennies to build up the economy, when the entire nation is making an effort, when all the construction workers labor nine and ten hours, when all the workers are giving us a percentage of their income for the industrialization of our country, at the very time that international cables are arriving with predictions that part of our sugar quota is going to be taken away. Diaz Lanz plans his aerial attacks and Huber Matos interrupts the ASTA Convention with his treacherous and criminal plan. These are the ways they try to block the Revolution's progress they ways they try to destroy the Revolution. By using economical threats and by thwarting our plans for developing our country. That is why when our people make such great sacrifices to gain one inch or one foot, it is unfair that these wretched conspirators destroy in minutes all that we have accomplished with such difficulty. What these miserable traitors want to do is to strangle the economy of Cuba, and spread terror among us until they succeed in making our nation fail. But I ask myself: What are they trying to do? Do they suppose that the revolution is not going to be defended? Do the Trujillos, the war criminals, the traitors, the foreign monopolies and the enemies of Cuba, believe that the revolution is not going to defend itself? Don't they understand we have the support of every farmer in Cuba? Don't they understand that we have the support of every worker in Cuba? Don't they understand that nobody is going to make the people of Cuba fall back? The people know very well who are their friends and who are their enemies. Don't the conspirators understand that the people of Cuba cannot even be confused? Every day the people know more and every day they are wider awake. Why do the conspirators get together and plot? Why do they drop bombs? Why do they plant hand-made bombs? Why do they openly elaborate their

Fidel Castro Speaks

counterrevolutionary campaigns? Simply
because they know they are running no risk.
They know that now, because of the respect
and generosity shown by the Revolutionary
Government, it is not dangerous to conspire.
They know of our efforts to carry out our
Revolution with complete kindness: they know
of our efforts to carry out our Revolution without
using "strong rule" tactics against the enemies
of the Revolution. This has encouraged them.
They know they are taking no risks. That is why
they conspire. That is why they come from
Santo Domingo and land in Trinidad. That is
why our troops find certain uprisings led by men
who are not Cuban. That is why our enemies
drop bombs, that is why they cause 47 victims in
our defenseless country--because they think
that our people are defenseless, because we
discontinued the trials by Revolutionary courts.
That is, they take unscrupulous advantage of
the generosity of our Revolution. Little does it
matter to them that 90% of all Cubans support
the Revolution. They are ready to machine--gun
the people, and bomb the people--to destroy the
people (if necessary and if possible). And every
day they have more gall. Every day they are
more insolent. On the very front pages of the

newspapers, they hide behind a woman's petticoats to write more or less that the Prime Minister is a criminal. What they never dared to publish against the dictator, what they never published against the government during the tyranny, they write against a man whose army was the first in the world ever to conduct a war without allowing a single prisoner of war to be killed, the first army in the world never to leave a single wounded enemy soldier on the battlefield, the first blockaded army--surrounded and blockaded for two years--to deprive their own soldiers of medicines in order to share their medicines with the enemy wounded. So every day with more nerve, with more gall, the reactionaries contrive to create confusion, to instigate treason, to whitewash the traitors and to aid and abet the unworthy men who abandon the cause of their people to serve the enemies of their people. They so dare because they know how great an interest we have in bringing the affairs of the nation back to normal. They know of our interest in developing the economy of our country. They see that we are striving desperately to find work for our people, to industrialize our country, with no assistance other than that of our own people. They see us

Fidel Castro Speaks

struggling heroically against giant foreign interests and they do not want us to win the battle. They do not want us to be able to concentrate all our energy on the revolutionary reform program. They want to destroy the revolution with their terrorism and by means of economic strangulation. But the revolution is not just mine; the revolution belongs to the people and we are doing nothing but carry out the will of the people. Now that is has become imperative, now that is has become a duty, to defend the revolution, it is the people who will have the last word. Now, with all our countrymen gathered together here, I an going to ask the people whether we should resume trials by the revolutionary courts... I want the people to express their opinion and to decide this matter. Those who are in favor of reestablishing the revolutionary courts should raise their hands. Since it is necessary for us to defend our country against aggression, since it is necessary to defend our country from aerial attacks from foreign bases, since it is necessary to defend our country against treason, the Council of Ministers will meet tomorrow to discuss and approve the law re-establishing war tribunals for as long as they are necessary. And

Fidel Castro Speaks

even though the courts will be the ones to decide according to law the sentence of each of the guilty, I want the opinion of the people. Please raise your hands those who think that the invaders of our country deserve to face the firing squad... Raise your hands, those who believe that the terrorists deserve to face the firing squad... Raise your hands, those who believe that pilots who fly over our territory and drop bombs on our people deserve to be condemned to death... And please raise your hands those who believe that traitors like Huber Matos deserve finally to face the firing squad. Everybody knows that we did our best to put an end to the war tribunals. Everybody knows the grief we were caused by the defamatory campaign made against our country while we were punishing the guilty. Everybody knows the efforts we have made to increase the tourist trade to develop the source of income for the country as part of the peaceful development of Cuba's wealth to feed the Cubans, to give them jobs. Everybody knows what a great effort we are making to carry our revolution forward, with the maximum of generosity, with the maximum of tolerance, with the maximum of good will. Everybody knows how we dislike having to give

Fidel Castro Speaks

again to the gang of base individuals who try to belittle us, to the international wire services, and to certain magazines and newspapers who slander us, another opportunity to present us before the world as callous and cruel. Everybody knows how much we sacrifice by re-establishing war tribunals and even the harm that will result to our economy, especially after that wonderful convention of the American Society of Travel Agents here. After thousands of our people worked so hard to make the convention a success, all the benefit we expected from it becomes no more than a vanishing illusion thanks to the traitors, the criminals of war, and the other enemies of Cuba. Everybody knows how hard and difficult it is for us to make this decision. But since we must defend our country from aggression, since we are being bombed, since our enemies want to defeat us by terror and hunger, we have no other alternative but to defend our country. We are men who do our duty. Cuba must, first of all, survive as a nation and defend her sovereignty as a nation. To survive is the matter of most urgency and must take precedence even over our most worthy illusions, even over our fondest dreams. We have always envisioned a future in

Fidel Castro Speaks

which we can bring about an era of peace and happiness. We have always dreamed of alleviating the pain and misery of the forgotten, of educating the uneducated, of feeding the hungry. We have always looked forward to providing the essentials of life to those who have always been the forgotten ones here in Cuba, those whom we remembered, when nobody else remembered them. While others spoke of democracy and of freedom they forgot that where there is ignorance, where there is hunger, and where there is despair, one should speak not of democracy but of oppression. Many Cubans have been held all their lives under the oppression of the big monopolies and robber barons. The first right of man is the right to life itself, the first right of man is the right to bread for himself and his children, the first right of man is to live by the sweat of his own brow; and all men are entitled to be given an education. Here the children of rural families died for lack of medical assistance; these children had no rights. Women became old before their time and died prematurely; these women had no rights. Entire families fainting from hunger had no rights. These Cubans were denied the right to life itself. The men who

Fidel Castro Speaks

deceived our people by making false use of abstract ideas always ignored those who make up the majority of our people, those for whom no one ever did anything, for whom no one ever fought, those whom we set out to redeem without taking the essentials of life from anybody else, those whom we are going to redeem by developing the wealth and resources of our own country. It is our dearest wish to bring relief to these people. We have dreamed and we will continue to dream of a revolution in which the will of the majority of the people may prevail over the selfish minorities. Greed on the part of the selfish minorities is what makes them unable to adapt themselves to the revolution which is a reality in Cuba today. We have dreamed that the great majority who support us would be respected by the minority. Instead, we have harvested counterrevolutionary campaigns, mercenary invasions, uprisings led by foreigners, aerial attacks from bases in foreign countries, and unscrupulous opposition by newspapermen who misuse freedom of the press to whitewash traitors in a concerted scheme of sabotage against us. As a consequence we have harvested the bombing of sugar mills and the destruction of homes in

Fidel Castro Speaks

the country and 47 victims in the capital. But we
are not willing to permit terror to take over the
country. With Santo Domingo on one side and
Florida on the other side, we are not willing to sit
idly by while every mother, every son, and every
wife, from one end of the island to the other,
lives as I saw families live in the Sierra Maestra-
-with a veritable psychosis about airplanes, in a
state of terror from bullets and bombings. We
must defend our country. Since we must defend
our people, since we must defend our school
children--the same children that I saw parading
and singing on their way to this impressive
concentration--since we must defend them;
since we have been harvesting only evil; and
since our enemies have become so audacious,
it is good for us to let the world know that the
Cuban people have decided to defend
themselves. Before the Cuban people are
anihilated, the Cuban people are ready to
anihilate as many enemies as are sent against
them. Before allowing themselves to be
murdered, the Cuban people are ready to die
fighting. The reactionaries, the invaders, and the
counterrevolutionaries, both inside Cuba and
outside Cuba, whether numerous or few, will
find a nation that is proud to declare that we do

Fidel Castro Speaks

not wish to do harm to anyone; that we do not
wish to jeopardize any other people in any part
of the world; that we wish only to live by our own
labor; we wish only to live from the fruits of our
own intelligence and wish only to live by the
work of our own hands, but in order to defend
our aspirations; in order to fulfill our destiny in
this world; in order to defend rights that are the
inalienable rights of any people of the world, big
or small, today, yesterday or tomorrow, in order
to defend our honest aspirations, the Cuban
people are ready to fight. Men, women, children,
even the aged, we are all ready to fight. Ours is
a just cause, we do not wish harm to anyone,
and no one has the right to do us harm. Today
we proclaim that we do not fear anything or
anyone, that we do not fear the measures taken
against us, and that we are not afraid to take all
the measures we may have to take against
those who wish to destroy us. Today Cuba has
attracted the attention of the whole world. Cuba
has won admiration all over the world and we
are not going to lose or abandon the respected
position we occupy among the peoples of Latin
America and the other people of the world.
Cuba is not going to be unworthy of the glory
and prestige we have gained by defending our

Fidel Castro Speaks

legitimate rights. Our revolution has been a success because of the kind of people you are. Otherwise, we could not carry out this kind of revolution. Those who have never studied history, and those who forget the history of other nations, those who have never read the chronicles of mankind, from the times of Greece to the present day, are the only ones who can fail to understand what a revolution is, and are the only ones who can be unaware that anybody who attempts to block a revolution will be crushed under the people's advance. Only those who are ignorant of history fail to understand that the hesitant and the cowardly are carried along by the people. Cuba is the scene of one of the most interesting and extraordinary revolutionary processes ever known, if we take into account the obstacles that must be overcome, if we take into account the powerful resources that are being used to crush our revolution. The people of Cuba have a mission to fulfill and we will fulfill it, because the people of Cuba are the kind with whom a revolution like this can be carried out. Those who lack the courage of their convictions are not important. When have they been important in the history of a nation? Those who hesitate do not matter.

Fidel Castro Speaks

When have they mattered in the history of a people? The cowards do not matter. When have the cowards mattered in the history of a people? When we were only twelve men, what did it matter that some hesitated and some lacked the courage of their convictions? Did they prevent the revolution from attaining an extraordinary victory? Twelve men finally succeeded in bringing the rest of the nation into the struggle. Today Cuba is holding her head high. Today Cuba fears no obstacle. This entire revolutionary nation is now on her feet and must not fear anything or anyone. The whole nation holds her head high like one great united army above those contemptible men who try to create confusion, above those unscrupulous ones who try to divide Cuba and weaken Cuba. Men of no feeling, they are unable to share in this hour of illusion the emotion or the spirit (that has been aroused) in Cuba after four centuries of struggling for justice. High above those who try to weaken it, the Nation stands united and disciplined like a single army. The people of Cuba are proud as a people. The nation is proud of its destiny. The people of Cuba are thinking as a nation for the first time, and united in a great cause. Those who are against Cuba

Fidel Castro Speaks

are all those who are unable to understand this great cause that has been undertaken by our nation, by our guajiro soldiers, by our farmers-- who constitute one half of our social group. Cuban workers, Cuban students, professional men and women of Cuba, and all other worthy Cubans of all walks of life, are aware that the fate of our nation is at stake. Our every survival as a nation is at stake. In order to attain peace and happiness, and well aware that our nation is involved in a heroic struggle that can free us from the bonds of economic and political slavery, the people of Cuba are determined to win these final battles in the struggle that began in the past century. The nation is convinced as it has never before been convinced that it is upholding a just and good cause. The nation is convinced of our loyalty, the nation is convinced that from this struggle there can be no retreat for us and we shall not retreat. The nation knows that we will not give up the fight until our bodies are laid to rest. The nation is conscious of its destiny, certain of its rights, proud of its History. When I see the emotion that shows on the face of all our people, I can have no doubt that Cuba will emerge victorious, because I firmly believe that a nation such as ours has become must be

Fidel Castro Speaks

respected. Nothing can dismay us now; we will not let accusations stop us; we are not concerned for our own lives; we care only about the destiny of our nation. The trust and faith placed in us by the people will not be betrayed, will not have been in vain. We are very conscious of our duty at this hour, and we can assure that we will do our duty. And just as, in the past, we assured you that the victory would be ours, we assure you now that if, as a nation, we can go ahead as we have begun, we will overcome our obstacles, because when the people of a nation are willing to fight for their rights, are ready to die, they must be respected. Those who preach fear are our worst enemies, those who preach fear are preaching our destruction, those who preach fear preach the extermination of our people. Get thee behind us! we say to the cowards. Get thee behind us! we say to the fainthearted. Get thee behind us! we say to all those who are trying to further their own petty ambitions in this, Cuba's finest hour. Get thee behind us! we say to all those who board the victory train when all goes well and abandon it at the first sign of trouble. Those who have courage, we invite to stay with us. Those who have faith, we invite to stay with us. Those

Fidel Castro Speaks

who are ready to give all they have, we invite to
stay with us. Anyone who lacks courage,
anyone who has doubts, should lose no time in
leaving the ship. Let the cowardly recant, let
those who have no faith recant. Those who
have a sense of duty do not fail in it. Those who
have a fighting spirit do not renounce it. Those
who do not feel able to play a role in this unique
moment in our history, should go their way.
Those who do not believe in the Revolution
should go their way. We believe in the people
and we know that the people will (justify our
belief, in them). Any government true to the
people, will find the people true to the leaders of
that government. It is not without meaning that
this rally is bigger than the one we held 8
months ago. It is not without meaning that after
10 months of Revolutionary Government the
people of Cuba give even greater support to the
revolution. The reason is simply that the
Revolutionary Government has been true to the
people. To all those who said that the
Revolutionary Government was going to grow
weak and lose favor we say: Look at the people,
and you will see that only the men who betray
the people lose their strength; the men who
remain loyal to the people never lose the

Fidel Castro Speaks

people's favor. What we want to point out is the progress of the revolution. What we want to point out is that every day we are given more co-operation. What must not be overlooked is that soldiers are building highways and schools, that teachers are working for half salary, that workers are voluntarily increasing their working-day to help the government, that citizens are collecting dollars, that children are collecting pennies, that workmen are working on Sundays to contribute their labor as a donation to the resources of the revolution. The wonderful spirit of self-abnegation on the part of the people, the stirring of the conscience of the people, the willingness to sacrifice whatever is necessary, the conviction that their destiny can be won by sacrifices, the certain knowledge that they themselves--and only they--can guarantee a better future and that they must rely on themselves, and the realization that heroic peoples are the only ones who have the right to be free, to be happy and to be independent: All this is what encourages us. It is heartening for us to see that our people are ready to make whatever sacrifice necessary, that they have the courage to cope with any risk that arises, and have courage enough to let our enemies know

Fidel Castro Speaks

that if they come, that if they drop bombs, and if they fire their guns at us in attacks upon us, the nation will be defended as long as a drop of blood remains in any of our people. Cuba will never surrender, every house will be a fortress; we will fight on every terrain necessary and with all kinds of weapons, and those who plot to take over Cuba will--as Maceo used to say--find only dust mixed with blood. So, if we cannot buy planes, we will fight on the ground when the fight comes down to the ground. If they persist in dropping bombs, we will build underground shelters and tunnels. The people are in a fighting mood, and we shall immediately begin training the farmers and the workers and the students. The tribunals of war and the Revolutionary military courts will be re-established and the pilots who land on Cuban territory will inexorably go before the firing squad. We will defend our country by fighting on every terrain necessary, and if England does not sell us the planes, we will buy them where they will sell them to us. If there is no money (in the treasury) to buy combat planes, the people will (give the money to) buy planes. And right here, right here, my friend Almeida, I give you the pay checks of the President of Cuba and of the

Fidel Castro Speaks

Prime Minister, as a contribution to buy planes. In closing, I want only to say: The Land Reform is here to stay. The Petroleum Law is here to stay. The Mining Law is here to stay. The Revolutionary measures taken to defend Cuba are here to stay. The Education Reform is here to stay. The Reform of the University and all our reforms are here to stay. If anybody wants to criticize us for this, let them criticize us. If they accuse us, (for this) let them accuse us; if they attack us, (for this) let them attack us. We shall fight those who dare plan the destruction of the revolution. And we take an oath in the name of the people of Cuba --that is, in the name of you and us-- that either Cuba will triumph or we shall all die (striving toward that triumph). Now, more than ever, we take for our own the words of our national anthem: "Hasten to the fight Cubans, the country is proudly watching: do not fear a glorious death. To die for your country is to live on".

Fidel Castro Speech to Congress
This is the first congress in revolutionary Cuba. It is the first meeting after many years of struggle and sacrifice in a completely free gathering. Many compatriots have fallen in the

Fidel Castro Speaks

struggle. An equally large number have had to suffer all kinds of humiliation and physical torture to achieve this. Much blood has been shed to make it possible today for the workers to hold this congress. It is not a congress attended by puppets only. The delegates present here were designated by the workers and the views expressed here are the freely expressed views of the workers. Decisions made here will be the expression of the free will of the Cuban workers. This must necessarily be a reason for pride for all of us. For seven years the working class was ruled by terror methods of the tyranny in complicity with trained accomplices serving the worst enemies of the people. For seven years the working class was not allowed to parade on May 1. (Applause). These were sad years which are gone forever. (Applause). Those who believe we will forget the past are mistaken. (Applause) The working class, which for seven years could not parade on May 1, has, by its efforts by its triumph since Jan. 1 become the decisive factor in the political life of the country, because it was the working class which in the general strike, promoted in conjunction with the rebel army, prevented efforts to snatch victory away at the last moment. It was the working

Fidel Castro Speaks

class which in these 10 months of revolution has been in the front lines,as it was in the first gathering of a million Cubans, as it was on May 1. Cuban workers protested the criminal attack on the national territory by planes from abroad. (Applause). Finally, it was the workers who organized the Oct. 27 rally. Whenever the workers have been called on, they have answered with enthusiasm and unity (Applause). This is a disciplined army which always answers "present" and is in the front ranks. It is the workers who have contributed most generously to buy tractors, to contribute to a day's work to our agrarian reform, to make their contribution to the defense of the sovereignty of the country, to buy arms to defend the national territory. Never has it failed the revolution. We have asked sacrifices of the workers. We know today that when the day comes when it may be necessary to defend the revolution by arms we shall turn to the workers. The destiny of Cuba and of the revolution is in the hands of the working class (applause) and it is vitally important that the working class understand that it holds the future of the country in its hands. The destiny of Cuba could not be in better hands. Fortunately, we can also count on

Fidel Castro Speaks

another sector of the nation, the Cuban campesinos (applause). The campesinos and working class need each other fighting side by side. In view of the threats and maneuvers by those who want to bring down upon them the yoke of privilege and injustice, what can they do against the united campesinos and workers? Of what use would it be for them to try to take back power against our united workers and campesinos? Against our soldiers, the campesinos, and workers with arms? Anyone who makes a mistake now is either irresponsible or stupid and unable to understand his own interests and the interests of the enemies of the country. if the workers should be defeated they would be made to pay a terrible price for freeing themselves from centuries-old evils. The people must be saved. Not only do we have the revolution's military with the workers and campesinos, but also most of the intellectuals. They are defending the interests of the people of Cuba. Enemies of Revolution Who will be against the revolution? Those whose interests are not the interests of Cuba and the Cuban people. The frustrated, those who sell themselves, those who betray, all those who conceived the revolution as a satisfaction of

Fidel Castro Speaks

personal ambition, not a people's undertaking, will be against the revolution, as well as all those who wanted to continue the past. When you analyze those who write against the revolution you will realize they serve the big interests, the enemies of the revolution. When you analyze the antirevolution press you will understand that a press developed by paid subsidies is the enemy of the revolution. The revolution has destroyed privileges. Those enjoying the privileges are against the revolution. Those who lack ideals are against it. In the early days of the revolution, when we spoke of latifundists, exploiters, war criminals, and Trujilloists, some thought we were exaggerating. It was difficult then to conceive that some of those who wrote little articles in favor of the revolution when it triumphed would joint those elements. Scarcely a few months had passed when we found a small group of latifundists associated not only with war criminals, but with a foreign tyrant who has been maintaining a bloody rule in his country for 30 years--Trujillo. Today it is evident that there is a connection between reactionary foreign press charges--between those who say there is no freedom of the press and those who receive

Fidel Castro Speaks

prizes from certain international organs (not specified--Ed.). One of these shameless ones has written an article "Lenin and Cuba." All agree on imputing to the revolutionary government the same charges. They insinuate that this is a foreign revolution (applause) when they themselves are the real supporters of foreigners. They come here to quote cables manufactured abroad against us and lies invented abroad against our revolution. They are defending the worst foreign interests. (Applause) The measures taken by the revolutionary government and the agrarian reform will recover more than 800,000 caballerias of land in the hands of a group of foreign countries to deliver it to the campesinos who live in hunger in our canefields. (Applause) Is this serving foreign interests? Is defense of the people against monopoly serving foreign interests, or a measure such as reducing the cost of electricity, putting an end to gambling and exploitation of the people, rice production (applause), protection of currency, customs measures, school construction, a clean administration, investment in public works instead of putting money into New York or Swiss banks, establishing justice (applause)--are these

Fidel Castro Speaks

serving foreign interests? I ask the people: Are the measures taken by the revolutionary government just? (Applause) if we are to be fought for taking just measures, let us be fought? If we must be invaded for this, let us be invaded. Our just revolution fulfills an historic mission. Can it be said after 10 months of government that there has been a single minister who has grown rich in office? The revolutionary government cannot be charged with promoting gambling, traffic in drugs, vice-- all traditional evils in our country. it is enough to read a cable such as I received here at this congress. It reveals enemies of our country. The cable reads: Washington, Nov. 18--There is evidence that in Cuba a rocket launching base is being established which could destroy Cape Canaveral and even the Pentagon, says Emilio Nunez Portuondo (Boos) in a weekly Latin American publication which is again circulating here. Almost all comment by Nunez Portuondo attacks our government and alleges dangers of communism. I am convinced, he says, that Cuba is becoming as dangerous for U.S. security as any captive country of East Europe. Thus they openly promote a policy of foreign intervention in our country. To justify this, they

Fidel Castro Speaks

invent tales such as this ridiculous story. What
and whom do reactionary press insinuations
serve? In articles such as one yesterday, titled:
"Lenin and Cuba," they simply tend to promote
foreign intervention. The problem is clear. You
must think as workers, campesinos, as Cubans.
(Applaud) Our strength lies in our identification
with the revolution. Is there a single worker who
does not agree with us? (Applause). The
revolution stands above all. This is the party of
the country. (Applaud). It is justice which unites
comrades, it is patriotic ideals which unite us.
When a criminal bomb falls over a district of
Cuba, or when terrorists and bandits carry out
acts, they do not discriminate or ask on which
house it is going to fall, or what Cuban it is going
to kill. The enemy who unites forces us to unite.
This is our strength. The spectacle which would
most please our enemies is any division in this
labor congress. (Applaud) They fear the
tremendous strength of the working class. They
know that it is invincible. They are going to listen
carefully to the congress to see whether there
are problems of difficulties. This means it is the
duty of all of us to see that this congress is an
example of revolutionary unit. (Applaud) We
know of the plans made to turn certain social

Fidel Castro Speaks

groups against us. We can see how they are trying to set one social group against another. They have no inkling of the revolutionary fevers which nowadays affect Cuban workers and farmers. (Applaud) These privileged groups are incapable of realizing that the measures which have affected certain privileged classes are the same which have brought hope and happiness to the immense majority of our people. The Enemy's Power Despite the injustices and nonsense which motivates them, they are still powerful. It is a struggle between those who possess it all and those who possess nothing. The same group who had a monopoly on the wealth of the country also possessed a monopoly of the means of publicity and information. They have the wealth necessary to lie around conspiring against the revolution. Their strength lies not in their numbers but in their resources and cunning. They also possess the education which the immense majority of our people lacks. The revolution is attacked by these privileged circles because it is trying to wipe out social ills and raise the social standards of the masses. In the face of aggression by these groups we have only one alternative--to unite farmers and workers in

Fidel Castro Speaks

order to defend the revolution. There must be discipline in the army of workers. You are the officers and leaders of that army. We must maintain the strength necessary to defend this revolution which will continue to forge ahead to its goals if we know how to defend it. When each farm, factory, household, ship, is a bulwark of the revolution, who will be able to defeat it? We must be aware that we will be attacked and that we shall have to defend it. Camilo was of the people just like you (applause). Our revolution had many men who were ready to die. They did not have any education, yet they knew their duty. It would have been logical that those fighters would have passed into government offices once the revolutionary cause was victorious. However they were not equipped for it. However, in the future they will be able to serve. This demonstrates the difficulties we face, but it also shows that in the long run victory will be ours. The Workers' Contribution Our most difficult task now is that of defending the revolution. Without a revolutionary government there can be no revolutionary program. I was very impressed by the resolution of the workers to contribute four percent of their earnings for the purchase of farm machinery.

Fidel Castro Speaks

This shows what the workers have learned.
They know that this is their government. They
know that the agrarian reforms affects precisely
that part of our economy which we can improve.
Our rice and cotton production this year will be
great. We must be able to meet our consumer
needs. We have invested much money in
agricultural production. The more we produce
on all types of necessary articles, the sooner our
living standard will rise. Our strategy must be to
put all unemployed to work. In this way I am
such we will reach our goals. The four percent
the worker gives now represents an investment
he will enjoy later. He will receive (bonds?)
which will not be redeemable for five years. The
worker not only will receive more from his
investment but will also enjoy a rising standard
of living. These sacrifices will repay us three or
four-fold. We are going to undertake the task of
training you as soon and rapidly as we can
(applause). Former governments here had large
armies to protect the privileges and investments
of the wealthy landholders. Who was then in a
position to do anything for the farmers? Nobody!
Now, on the other hand, the farmers are being
defended against the large landholders. The
same applies to the workers. They have won

Fidel Castro Speaks

their rights. The privileged classes tremble--they know that their privileges are a thing of the past. Let them return if they dare, but they will find an armed Cuba awaiting them--and armed Cuba which will defend its hard-won rights. Foreign Lies You know the efforts of foreign news agencies to subvert the revolutionary government. They continue to print lines and slander. You can imagine how it hurts us to read those slanderous lies about Camilo Cienfuegos. We shall always keep the people abreast of the news and latest slanderous and subverting campaigns of our enemies so that they will know the truth. To be a revolutionary is to have the courage to face the truth. The efforts and sacrifices of the people have not been in vain. They did it once and will do it again, as many times as necessary. We shall take care of each problem and difficulty as it arises. If the rich antirevolutionaries begin to conspire, the farmers and workers are lined up, ready to defend the revolution. We can say with certainty that none of their maneuvers, will succeed here.

Fidel Castro Speech on Military
The question we must ask ourselves following the ceremony this morning, following this

Fidel Castro Speaks

spectacle of thousands and thousands of children with Cuban flags in the military parade ground of the former Ignacio Agramonte Regiment, following this moving and unforgettable ceremony -- this is the question we must ask: what need did the revolution have for this military fortress? For what does the revolution need military fortresses? What governments needed military fortresses? Only governments which do not work for the people, only governments which defend interests opposed to those of the people, need military fortresses. But we, the revolutionary government, the actions of which we all absolutely to the benefit of the people, why do we need military fortresses? For what did a military fortress serve? The fortresses were the refuge, the lodging of an army which was not in the service of the people. What was the army in our fatherland? What role did the army play in Cuba in the past? It was an organization in the service of the great interests, an organization trained and equipped to defend the great interests and the great interests needed an army to defend them. Did that army exist to defend the people? Whom did it defend? The great interests. That army did not defend the republic. That army did not defend the people. That army existed to keep the people in the clutches of the established interests and the privileged. For a trifle they raised those guns which so often struck and fired upon our compatriots. For a trifle they raised those swords which so often fell on the shoulders of our citizens. And today, whom can those machetes, which are all in the hands of the peasants themselves, strike? In the past it was the peasants who received the blows. The fact that problems were resolved with machete blows is a truth which our people, particularly our peasants, know only too well. But today, who has the machetes in hand? The rural people have ceased to be those who receive the blows, they have ceased to be the victims, to become defenders of their revolution, machetes in hand. And who could ever reestablish that hateful system in our fatherland? Who could ever deal a single blow again to a single one of the peasants in our fatherland? How could it be possible for our peasants to let themselves become victims of such injustice again? Then... why fortresses? What need has the revolution to maintain a fortress full of soldiers, if these fortresses were built precisely to subject the people, if these fortresses were built to abuse the people? Thus the revolution needs no fortresses. This is why the revolutionary government promised the people that it would convert the fortresses into school cities, and this in Camaguey is the second fortress we have converted into a school city. Next will come one in Holguin, then the Moncada Barracks in Santiago de Cuba, and then the military fortress in Santa Clara. And thus, the revolutionary government of Cuba will be the first government in the world to convert military fortresses into schools. But there is something else. What better proof could be given of trust in the revolution? What better proof could be given of faith in the people? Because the revolution is converting fortresses into schools just when more enemies are emerging everywhere against our revolution, just when more threats to our revolution are coming from all sides, just when the campaign of the reactionaries and the great interests against our revolution is boldest and most aggressive. Nonetheless, far from building fortresses, what the revolution is doing is to destroy fortresses to make them into schools. Why? Is is perhaps that the revolution will remain defenseless? No. Is it perhaps that we

Fidel Castro Speaks

are going to disarm? No. What is happening is that we have understood the problem perfectly; before there were armies to oppress the people, and now the people constitute the best army of the republic. Now the defenders of the republic are the citizens themselves. Why can the revolution convert fortresses into schools? Because since 1 January, since the triumph of the revolution, each school has become a fortress of the revolution, and the 10,000 schools which will be established by the revolutionary government in the course of this year will be 10,000 fortresses of the revolution. Because each city, each village, each home has become a fortress of the revolution. Despite the fact that it is destroying fortresses, Cuba is better defended than ever, and the revolution is better defended than ever, because the people are defending it. This means that the revolution has in the people its most legitimate defender. The revolution has in the people its best army, and when the time comes to defend the revolution and the fatherland, each citizen, each compatriot, will be a soldier of the revolution and the fatherland. Could any other government train the peasants and arm the peasants, the workers and the students? No. Why? Because if

Fidel Castro Speaks

the workers and the peasants and the students and the people had been armed, Cuba would not have suffered under dictatorship, under evil governments. Evil governments were possible only because those were armies in the service of the great interests. The best proof of the fact that the revolution means the complete identification of the government in the people is that the government is placing the defense of the revolution in the hands of an army. There are many things we would like to say to the people of Camaguey, but since the circumstances do not allow me to go on at length what I would like to say is thank you! Than you for this unprecedented support! Thank you for this turnout, such as we have never before seen in our lives! Thank you, because this is the most significant manifestation given in favor of the revolution. Because if we take into account the number of inhabitants in this province, we can say that a larger proportion than those who have turned out in any other place in Cuba have come to support the revolutionary government. The attendance of a crowd which stretches for more than a kilometer along this avenue is a spectacle so impressive that note of us will ever be able to forget it. It is a

Fidel Castro Speaks

spectacle which will remain engraved in our minds as a concept of what Camaguey is, as an idea of the revolutionary nature of the people of Camaguey, as an idea of how loyal the people of Camaguey are, how valiant they are. And for this we say thank you! The enemies of the revolution are gathering, the enemies of the revolution are organizing, the enemies of the revolution are increasingly daring and more insolent in their campaigns against the revolution. There is a still more terrible firing law for the reactionaries. The firing law which frightens the counterrevolutionaries most is not that at which the firing squads aim. The firing law which terrifies the counterrevolutionaries most is the people, the firing law of the people. What frightens the reactionaries most is the machetes which are brandished by our peasants. What frightens the reactionaries most is the vast multitude which has gathered here today and which is saying to the counterrevolutionaries, which is saying to the ruffians, which is saying to the estate owners, which is saying to the profiteers and the privileged that they must abandon hope, because oppression, injustice, exploitation, estate owning, plunder, vice, crime and the

Fidel Castro Speaks

sadness of our people, the humiliation, will not return. The blows to the peasants and the citizens will not come again, nor will those who plunder the wealth of our people, now will the domination of the monopolies, of foreign interests, nor will foreign intervention in our politics or treasonable governments return. Nor will the nefarious policy the counterrevolutionaries want, nor will the abolished privileges return, because in order for the past to return, it would first be necessary to exterminate our people. A better future will come. What our fatherland has never had will come. Full national sovereignty, schools, culture, work, wealth for our people, land for our peasants will come to stay and, whatever it may cost, a better future and a more honorable and more worthy life for all Cubans will come. Those who will never return are the hired ruffians. Those who will never again govern our fatherland are the counterrevolutionaries, because they know that the people like this can not be defeated. For this reason, in the name of the people themselves, because the only thing which concerns us, the only thing which interests us, is the future of this people, we express to the people today our recognition and

Fidel Castro Speaks

our gratitude, because once again we reaffirm the convictions that the people of Cuba are an extraordinary people, that they have a right to a glorious destiny, that with a people like this, we can go as far as we want. And for this reason we thank you, because you today, citizens of Camaguey, after 11 months of revolutionary government, have given the government greater support than it has ever had, you have given the revolutionary government an inspiration, a greater stimulus than it has ever had. And completing the first year of revolutionary government, after seeing the fruits of our laws, after seeing the results of our efforts, we can tell the people that we propose to undertake the second year of the revolutionary government, the second year of just laws and creative effort, the second year of work for the good of the people and the fatherland. And in continuing the work we have the same faith and the same decision as we have always had, because we need not render accounts for our work to anyone but the citizens of our fatherland. The struggle in recent years has been hard. Dearly beloved comrades have fallen. For example, Comrade Camilo Cienfuegos is not with us today, and it is with profound sorrow that we

Fidel Castro Speaks

remember him at this gathering, with infinite sadness because he cannot share with us this experience of turning over to the children the military fortress, and this moving sight of such an extraordinary and dense concentration of people. This is a hard path along which we often have to note the absence of comrades who, as he did, began this struggle with us. It is still harder to think that this comrade lost his life, as many of the posters say, fighting treason, a betrayal which has cost us dear, which meant for us the loss of Camilo Cienfuegos. And for this reason I admire our people still more, because the betrayal has not discouraged them. Nor are they discouraged by blows as harsh as the death of so glorious and useful a comrade as Camilo was for us, and thus our people are admirable because of the faith they have, which nothing discourages, because of their bravery, which nothing can daunt, because of their dedication, which neither wavers nor is diminished by anything. For this reason, the citizens of Camaguey have our eternal recognition and gratitude, this is the reason for the special sympathy I feel for this province, although I was not born here, and although all Cubans have equal value for me, whatever the

Fidel Castro Speaks

province in which they were born, and although I am an enemy of all regionalism. However, I could not fail to have a very profound feeling and a very special sympathy links me with the people of Camaguey, because I have the same faith in and sympathy with you that you have for us, the same confidence you have had in us, and the first impression I have on traveling through his province is one which has not changed and which has become increasingly firm. This is because that impression has never been altered by facts, and I believe that the links between the people of Camaguey and the revolutionary government are increasingly strong. The province in which according to all the surveys support has been greatest has been Camaguey, and I have seen that this revolutionary spirit, rather than diminishing, is growing, and is more ardent every day, more enthusiastic and firmer every day. For this reason, we love Camaguey, for this reason we have sympathy with Camaguey and for this reason we have confidence in Camaguey. And this has not been confidence in words, but confidence in deeds. I demonstrated this confidence in coming alone to deal, jointly with the people of Camaguey, with the treasonable

Fidel Castro Speaks

plot of an ambitious individual who wanted to perpetrate a criminal act against the revolution here. This means that our confidence in the people of Camaguey is not something about which we talk, but something we have demonstrated and will continue to demonstrate. Perhaps the reason for the extraordinary revolutionary spirit of the citizens of Camaguey is due to the fact that this was the province of the large estate owners, where there was the greatest injustice and the most social exploitation. But for this reason, took Camaguey will be the province in which the work of the revolution will go farthest, will be deepest, because revolutions are the greater and the more necessary where the injustices are the greater. I bid you farewell with this expression of sympathy and faith in the people of Camaguey. Perhaps on another occasion we can speak to you with less difficulty, perhaps on another occasion we will not have the technical problems we have had, and I can speak to you more easily. But in saying farewell, I want to tell you that thanks to you, we leave this province with redoubled energy, with redoubled faith and with redoubled enthusiasm with which to move forward. And also we depart with this thought --

Fidel Castro Speaks

that we can always count on the people of Camaguey, and the revolution will be able to count on them in the most difficult and hard days. With the people of Camaguey, the revolution will be able to fight the battles which may be necessary, and we can count on the people of Camaguey to the last breath and the last drop of blood. Camaguey will always be the loyal province it has been to date. The people will be loyal as they always have, and the example of Camaguey will be imitated by all Cubans in all the provinces of Cuba. And the people will be able to say to the little groups of reactionaries, of privileged persons who want to promote their counterrevolutionary spirit in the provinces: "Back, back, because the interests of the privileged strata, the interests of the little groups of powerful families are not the interests of the rural people, of the workers, of the fishermen, of the charcoal producers, of the humble men, nor of honorable citizens." Back, because the more you fight the revolution, the more people will support the revolution. Back, hypocrites, because you are not combating the revolution because it has been evil but because it has done good. You are not combating the revolution because it has done harm to the

Fidel Castro Speaks

people, but because it has done good for them. Back, hypocrites, who are battling the revolution because the revolution has been firm and not vacillating, because the revolution has been brave with regard to national and foreign interests and not cowardly. The people will be able to answer the gangs of hypocrites, the intriguers who, here as in Oriente, and as in other provinces, are battling the revolution, because the revolution has been courageous in destroying their privileges, courages in advancing itself and challenging their omnipotent power, the power they have exercised to date, because on 1 January the battle against the mercenary soldiers, against the hired ruffians, ended, but the battle against the privileged began, and we are engaged in this battle. And this triumph today is a part of this battle, a part of the triumph, because we are engaged in the battle against the privileged, which is a long and hard one, but one we will win, as we won the battle against the mercenaries and the ruffians. The people will block the advance of the plotters, the hypocrites, the privileged, and thus as I have met today with the people of Camaguey, I will meet on the 30th with the people of Oriente, and with the people

Fidel Castro Speaks

of Santiago. And there, too, the people will gather, while the privileged and the reactionaries contemplate their plots and their impotence, those who believe that this was a revolution of little lies, those who understood to toy with the revolution and now have found that it is a revolution of truth, and not of lies. And the people will gather, the rural people with their machetes, in Santiago de Cuba, and there, too, there will be an imposing gathering like this, to say to the plotters, to the hypocrites, "back!" And the people will gather there in Santiago de Cuba, as they have gathered here, to halt the maneuvers of the counterrevolutionaries, to impose, by their presence, by their enthusiasm, the respect the revolution merits, because if the gangs of the privileged had no idea of what a revolution is, they will learn that this is a true revolution and not a game. And the privileged must understand that their pain, when they see their hateful privileges destroyed, is not the pain of the people. The indignation of the privileged is not the indignation of the people, because the people, when privileges are destroyed, are inspired with hope, the people are filled with hope and happiness. The pain of the privileged is the happiness of the people, and the

Fidel Castro Speaks

destruction of privileges is the future of the fatherland and the happiness of the people. And thus, what I have said today, the words I have spoken here, I will say in Santiago and I will say to the people of Oriente, where we also have a loyal people who will be able to give the lie they deserve to the plotters and maneuverers of the counterrevolution. And we can also say to the people of Oriente what we have said to the people of Camaguey: that we can always count on the people of Oriente, as on the people of Camaguey, and that in order to triumph over the revolution it will be necessary first to annihilate the latest revolutionary, and that in our fatherland, it will be from these provinces that the forgers of its destiny will come, that its last defendants will come. In each of them, the first to takeup arms in our wars of independence will be the last to cease to fight when it is necessary to defend it. And for this reason we can say that the revolution is invincible, because we have this people. For this reason, we can state that the revolution will advance with the energy which is necessary, because we have a people such as this. It is for this reason that we are blending ever increasingly with the people, because we believed in them when no one did,

Fidel Castro Speaks

because we believed in them when the people were unarmed and powerless, and now events have borne us out. We have won the war and we are winning the peace. It is for this reason that we feel increasingly identified with the people, more closely linked with the people, because we believed in them when no one did. How could we not believe, seeing them free, powerful, united, seeing them advance, full of enthusiasms and bravery, to conquer the fatherland in which we believe? For this reason, we have faith in the ultimate victory, because if we had faith in those mountains, when we were no more than a handful of men, how can we fail to have faith today, when we are supported by an entire people, generous and brave, with whom we will fight the battles which are necessary, with whom we will wage the struggle against the great interests, however powerful they may be, which stand in our path, against the obstacles, however great they may be, which stand in our path. And we will triumph because this time Cuba will indeed achieve its destiny, and nothing and no one can prevent it from doing so. This time what happened in 68, in 95, in 33 will not happen. This time the Cuban

Fidel Castro Speaks

people will be able to win the laurels of the most complete victory.

MIKAZUKI PUBLISHING HOUSE™

(U.S.P.T.O. Serial Number 85705702)
1. 25 Principles of Martial Arts
2. 25 Principles of Strategy
3. American Antifa
4. American Bookstore Directory
5. Arctic Black Gold
6. Art of War
7. Back to Gold
8. Basketball Team Play Design Book
9. Bernie Sanders Revolution
10. Boxing Coloring Book
11. California's Next Century 2.0
12. Camping Survival Handbook
13. Captain Bligh's Voyage
14. Coming to America Handbook
15. Customer Sales Organizer
16. DIY Comic Book
17. DIY Comic Book Part II
18. Economic Collapse Survival Manual
19. Farrakhan Speaks
20. Fidel Castro Speaks
21. Find The Ideal Husband
22. Football Play Design Book
23. Freakshow Los Angeles
24. Game Creation Manual

Fidel Castro Speaks

25. George Washington's Farewell Address
26. GhostHuntTV Ghost Hunting Notebook
27. Hagakure
28. History of Aliens
29. Hollywood Talent Agency Directory
30. I Dream in Haiku
31. Internet Connected World
32. Irish Republican Army Manual of Guerrilla Warfare
33. Japan History Coloring Book
34. John Locke's 2nd Treatise on Civil Government
35. Karate 360
36. Learning Magic
37. Living the Pirate Code
38. Magic as Science and Religion
39. Magicians Coloring Book
40. Make Racists Afraid Again
41. Master Password Organizer Handbook
42. Mikazuki Jujitsu Manual
43. Mikazuki Political Science Manual
44. MMA Coloring Book
45. Mythology Coloring Book
46. Mythology Dictionary
47. Native Americana
48. Ninja Style
49. Ouija Board Enigma
50. Palloncino
51. Political Advertising Manual
52. Quotes Gone Wild

Fidel Castro Speaks

Facebook.com/MikazukiPublishingHouse

Fidel Castro Speaks

KAMBIZ MOSTOFIZADEH TITLES
1. 25 Principles of Martial Arts
2. 25 Principles of Strategy
3. American Antifa
4. American Bookstore Directory
5. Arctic Black Gold
6. Back To Gold
7. Camping Survival Handbook
8. Economic Collapse Survival Manual
9. Find the Ideal Husband
10. Game Creation Manual
11. GhostHuntTV Ghost Hunting Notebook
12. History of Aliens
13. Hollywood Talent Agency Directory
14. Internet Connected World
15. Karate 360
16. Learning Magic
17. Magic as Science & Religion
18. Make Racists Afraid Again
19. Mikazuki Jujitsu Manual
20. Mikazuki Political Science Manual
21. Mythology Dictionary
22. Native Americana
23. Ninja Style
24. Ouija Board Enigma
25. Political Advertising Manual
26. Saving America
27. Small Arms & Deep Pockets
28. Shinzen Karate
29. The Bribe Vibe

Fidel Castro Speaks

www.ingramcontent.com/pod-product-compliance
Lightning Source LLC
Chambersburg PA
CBHW072011290326
41934CB00007BA/1051